Melissa Lee-Houghton   *Exposure / Ideal Palace*

AF084517

P
A
R
I
A
H

EXPOSURE / IDEAL PALACE

MELISSA LEE-HOUGHTON

PARIAH PRESS · 2024

Exposure / Ideal Palace
Copyright © 2024 Melissa Lee-Houghton
ALL RIGHTS RESERVED

Published by PARIAH PRESS · 2024
pariahpress.com | pariah@gmail.com

British Library Cataloguing in Publication Data
Lee-Houghton, Melissa
Exposure / Ideal Palace
ISBN 978-1-9196296-1-2 paperback

Any edition of this book is sold subject to the condition that it shall not, by way of trade, be lent, resold, hired out, or otherwise disposed of, without the publishers' consent, in any form of binding other than that in which it is first published. No part of this publication may be reproduced, stored in a retrieval system, or transmitted in any form by any means, electronic, photocopying, mechanical or otherwise without prior permission of the copyright holder and publisher.

Pariah would like to thank the following people: Jelena Calic for the printing of the early proofs. Clare Conville and Cheerio Publishing for generous donations to aid the book's printing. Becky Wyde and Jonny Walsh for proofreading. Hal Hockney, Vik Shirley, Alex Wakefield, Dan Wakefield, and the many others who have aided in the process of reading, editing and decision making. And of course, thank you to Melissa.

Art direction & cover design by Adam Griffiths: ra-bear.com

Designed & typeset in Garamond Premier Pro by Luke Allan at Studio Lamont

Printed by CPI

Contents

❧ VOLUME I: EXPOSURE

Marriage in Seven Acts Each Containing Sadistic Lovers w/ Deafening Howls of Pleasure — 11

If You've Never Been Down You Have Never Seen Anything Like It — 13

Wash Your Mouth Out — 16

Solar Plexus — 17

My Late Father's Decline as Sunset Fell Over the Sea — 18

Come Back to Me — 19

Disappearing Incompletely — 20

Narcotise — 21

Desperately — 22

Nazi Soldiers Dream of Making My Day — 23

Imposters — 25

Reassuringly Bourgeois — 27

I'm Amazed — 28

One Eye Open — 30

Appulse — 31

Whitechapel after rain & then the long plateau — 32

Mobile Slaughter Hall — 34

Until The Last Light Goes Out I Was Still Here — 37

With Gun & Regret — 38

Battlespace — 41

Duplicity: A Letter — 44

Heroin — 51

Heroin II — 52

Letter: 'too lengthy a prose for such a bad one' 4th June 2017 — 53

Overshot — 54

This System Of Values Has No Get-Out Clause — 55

Indelible, and Surely There — 57

Solar Cycle Twenty-Four — 59

Transmigration of Souls — 63

Bleak Future Text — 65

Beelzebub Has No Truck With This International Court Judge Says Tearful Witness And Adds 'Thank God, Amen' — 67

And Anyway, In Light Of These Recent Events, I Don't Even Know Why I Came — 69

White Nights — 71

The Distant Mirror — 73

❧ VOLUME II: IDEAL PALACE

Psychorrhax — 85

A Comprehensive History of the Byzantine Church — 88

Hindmilk — 92

Me & You in Ulysses — 95

Galileo — 98

My Blue Beryl — 104

Manasa — 106

Clean Blue Night — 108

Original Mover — 111

Janus — 112

Parallax — 114

Obit in Suck Magazine 1969 — 115

Never Never Never — 119

Recapitulation — 122

Professional Vs Amateur Wrestling — 124

Reasonable Doubt — 128

Palos Verdes Blue — 131

My Telepathic Phonometrician — 133

V. A. Fogg — 138

Oh Hell — 139

Golden Palaces — 145

Caroline — 147

Blackout # 57 w/ Snow Drift and Premature Meteorite Burst — 149

Haint Blue — 151

Rhett Butler — 153

Bird-Watching — 155

Fatherland — 157

White Mist — 159

Slingers — 168

Apple Rain — 169

You've spent days in a world
Made possible by drink,
All thresholds and doors and beds
Where you closed your eyes.

KATY AISENBERG
Excavations

Somewhere our belonging particles
Believe in us. If we could only find them.

W.S. GRAHAM
Implements in Their Places

Exposure

VOLUME I

Marriage in Seven Acts Each Containing Sadistic Lovers w/ Deafening Howls of Pleasure

I shall touch everything with my senses and make even the static objects vibrate with lust. Please never resist me or learn from my mistakes—
there was a past time in which I was all throat and no joy but now I am all mouth and full-hearted the whole skin leans over the edge of your consciousness
threatens to jump and you catch me and all the words fall out and down into the pit. I'm so cat-like I'm a human failure, so glamorous lying in bed
in snakeskin platform sandals, sleeping through the afternoon lined with a sickeningly delicious sweat, all my glands aching and all my tunnels filling with poise.
Tunnel into my bed tonight or tunnel into my weaknesses, or tunnel into my despondencies, or tunnel into my inability to make prayers
I am sanctity itself my darling don't patronise me have you any idea how much brain it takes to make a fool out of you.

    Erroneously enterprising fluke, you walk out into the fray in fact you dance out, you push your way through a thicket of buffoons and then you
interrupt several people as they imagine they are a democracy of one. My daughter notes I seem not to notice physical pain. The emotional pain proliferates
so exuberantly it's hard to be anything other than a portal for all Hells and high waters. Saturn eating his sons becomes me eating a room full of sour auras
and spitting them into poems that turn on a rack through our outrage. I'm completely besotted with you; what do I expect you to do with that? Well,
you could have a good scan of my entire body until you hit on something you really like and make sure you exercise your right to make it sizzle with lack of control.
I get so out of control you barely have to touch me what's wrong with you I barely have to touch you and not that long ago a room full of male friends sat and
watched you spontaneously orgasm sat alone on a green velour couch. One of the kindest of them put his arm around you but my God what the hell was that.

    And Jim Jones rocks back and forth in a rocking chair on a podium made of milk-teeth, bares his teeth and shrieks *kill the children.*
There are no men who can bear you. You are able to milk a prostate from fifty feet. You are talented and go from emotionally overwrought
to street-smart in three seconds. Do entertain this; you will simply never have this much fun again. A chronic belief in the honourable nature of direct assault.
My senses touch on all things, all words fly into the heartcollapse of my feelings, I fly into the sensations and get no sleep. Reeling in a single bed of sexual
plight, a montage of psychoanalytic archetypes and every nerve nailed to its own architecture of I Want.

    As my stomach fills with a change-of-heart plus Valium I become faceless at the edges.
                  What makes you think of me. I never think of you.
I think of you all the time. You think of me often. You think of me when you're alone. You think of me when someone is boring. I think of you when
I'm seen. Get a long look now, I'm not coming back. Unimpressed by my inability to not press my mouth against his neck and push all of my
tense and volatile flesh against him as though I might dissolve or melt or cease to exist in essence or substance.

Now fuck off and fly over St Petersburg like the fragrant witch you are.
                        Be complicit in all complicity.
                        Laugh at your father's pre-intercourse and post-coital failings.
                        This time I win. I win.
                        Yes stretch your arms out like that so I can bury my face in your chest.
                        Stretch wide and be like the sunset just a shock of impulse raving over your lack of presence.

His hair comes away at the scalp in my grazed hand to memorialise the impulse to dissolve and be corroded.

        Yes I'm present to you in a way no one is. Yes well go back and say no more about it. Clasp my wrist in your sleep and pour
hot oil over my face. I am no more. I have gone down ingeniously. The neverending nature of true love is that it must be recognised to justify killing itself.
All these deaths and none of them ours, or mine, and I scar and stare into the pits of your eyes, a house situated in your psychic retentions, no one cares, and I can't
save you. She can save, I'm Mary Magdalene is all, and I heave with sobs over the apex of your ejaculations—yes, I can do almost anything and you want none.
Frying in a particular heat and everyone in London baking but not simmering quite as intensely as this little stallion I imagine I'm more masculine
than I am as a way through being feminine and no one wanting to bask in that. It's too hot for stockings but easy to have sex in public as we're barely clothed.
You are the worst most highly sexed person in this lockdown of literati and shame. The sauvignon blanc is really testing my will to live
the longer I stand here being impolite the more the stormcloud overhead can't be arsed. It's no secret I can't behave appropriately in times of intimacy-drought.
Just pat it or rub it a little bit, mmm like that, and don't stop or I might tear up the entire block with my superhuman libido.

For God's sake fuck her. 100%.
        Yes I have the veal and I'll dissuade your loyalty and your love when the time is most convenient.
        Piracy is a crime. I stole the prize-winning books. I couldn't plagiarise anything, it wouldn't cut it
you see what I did there, pretending my ego is stable and big and dismantling your sex drive. I will rip that earring out of your ear.
Wrap it round my throat. I adore you I adore you I adore you sleep fretfully and wake in the wrong bedsheet.
        Verily verily verily the cycles of my heartflare meet you nowhere as you realise my aim is perfectly malignant;
        mirrored glass in Mark's apartment. Jim rots in the next to last purgatory which is closer to sainthood than I—
I languish in full view of a wasteland, get bitten in the mouth by a stranger and float
        sipping sweet tea and meringue-like sickly panic attack look at this impetuous beaten-up thing
        tip of your tongue on the tip of my about-turn
        she has decided now to leave my darling you won't change her sharp decision making
        in a box full of precious things you unwrap the only object that could kill someone
        and it makes you feel just like you feel when she walks right up to you sinking into the décor
        tulip-witted and snake-like and what a time to be straddled by this tempestuous need

        for a paginated romantic
        traumatised
        over Vauxhall Bridge the sun came up and I missed seeing into it
        I saw so far beyond it you didn't even exist.

If You've Never Been Down You Have Never Seen Anything Like It

I haven't sucked anything for weeks. Ice lollies out of date by three years and
all those insecurities about boyfriends telling on your lack of technique, but it was technique
learned aged six and aged six your mouth is not a wide orifice.

I open the prosecco and toast him, he is in the city with his hard on making women
freeze on the spot in Soho with his unambiguous and war-drone cock hardening
in his black jeans at the thought of me and my undulating breasts as I masturbate furiously in the corner;

and you know no one else gets it. You know, don't you, that no one does.
You know that no one does and yet I am in love. The totality of me has a microchip so when
I can't get home they hone in and they replace me with someone better and send her back

and these baggy jumper dresses, these hard heels, these epilated legs, these wet knickers these
long drags on cold nights beckoning from a distance you, these what the fucks these
tall orders for penetration that can't come for me and these dead thighs procrastinating.

I'm happy for you, no, I'm ECSTATIC. I'm so PROUD of you they all want to suck you baby
you go HARD always go hard don't you know we all have an edge just most people plane it down
to make babies and coagulate in wholesome concepts. Our edge is hanging off the stained bed

like I hung off the edge of the stained bed passed out you saw me drained you
fed me hot chicken I sucked it off you reached out in the city and you saw wild animals
tamer than me. You said coochy. And they came and didn't bite like I bit. And yes you liked it.

There are so many lovers you haven't met yet. You have my picture, the one with the fishnet stocking
around my scarred neck. You have the cataracts I glazed over your eyes so you wouldn't see sex
and you have the essay I wrote for you about my love which you never read you didn't even skim it.

Exorcism doesn't work unless you have faith in a good/bad dichotomy. Oh our in-between places
are every shade of good/bad I want to wrestle you off the stage tonight and pour this drink
down your open throat and you open it and you open it. I am three years out of date

for this kind of tumult. *I'm not an adolescent* is just something a thirty four year old woman
should not have to say from a park bench at ten past eight on a Tuesday night whilst you tell me
'well, if you died tomorrow I'd be a bit upset.' But it was me you called.

I was high on pregabalin, codeine, tramadol and diazepam. All together not
in any way unenjoyable. I've decided to knock the drugs on the head. Drink, smoke, fuck.
I bleed in between periods, maybe I should take better care of my soft parts and maybe you should

live in an empty place because I am all sundown over your brittleness and you say in the pub
'why am I hard just talking to you?' I say, 'because I'm really fucking hot.' The poet says I'm trouble
but I'm all heart god damn it. This is how I bite a banana David, look. I peel back the skin, first, like this.

I put it in my aching mouth and hold it between my teeth for a second, are you watching? Good.
I settle my teeth into the flesh, see? Like this. And then it comes off clean into my mouth. You
are the best fuck I ever had you are a million Marilyn Monroes and I have no reason to love you.

My life is galloping off to another timezone; can you see it go? I can't come back to you to get blitzed again.
I had to wash in Costa and had nothing to dry myself with and as I was soaking wet someone came
as I drank a ridiculously oversized mug and asked if I was ok. I said, 'it's just the withdrawals, love.'

They wouldn't take the tags off my shoes in TK MAXX I said how can I walk around with tags
they said they didn't have scissors I nearly wet myself carrying those bags and you wouldn't
carry them for me a guy put his head out of the window of his car and shouted wanker at you

he said, 'carry her fucking bags' and you said you didn't want to live in Hackney anymore.
Relationship sabotage is so 1980s dude. I've washed since and I'm clean and I have lapped
and lapped at the milk and I have suffered without an audience would you even believe

and I have slept in several layers of unwashed clothes with no call coming through no sign.
I make a film of myself reading Sarah Kane. You will never see me cry unless you stop hurting me.
I wake up at three and five and hallucinate a man holding out a begging cup and both times

I've got nothing to put in. There's nothing left. All the milk gone, the cream ejaculated
licked at it I did. And it was sweet. And I was a fetish. An acquired taste, except I taste good
if you have a brain and that's all it needed. Oh your beautiful brain, how you held me after you came,

your beautiful, you're beautiful, you never said that you just said I had a *vibe*
but a vibe only gets you so far. At some point you have to concede that to be a fantasy you must
fail to meet it. This pussy, this heart, this bruise. A wide openness to pain, something to block the door

so the wild animals don't get in. The big girls look hot, you said. You'd never considered them before me.
So much flesh to tear up; and I smoked that cigarette slow enough for punishment. Hurry up.
I do everything too quick. It's like I need just that moment, and then I need

to get the fuck out of bed, out the room, out the head that encases me so untenderly.
So can you get it? Yeah. How much? I'm up for it. Temptation is a massive cock and it carries a hefty price tag
and I'm so aroused right now I might sit outside and smoke and look at the moon and pretend

I'm Betty Blue only I'm not. I'm just a human stain. I lick the paper, and feel the rain. Yes,
my darling, melancholia does suck.

Wash Your Mouth Out

He said, *can you afford the parachute?* I said, *not really*, he said, *good luck*.
I offered my book and she said, *how much is it worth?* and I said *practically nothing*.
She said *when you get the advance we'll negotiate*. I said *I don't know the value of money,* and thought,
but I do know the value of my vices. *It's a start,* she said, and shook her head.
    To centre myself, I tried hard to get lost in Brixton by just walking but the walking
brought me round rather poetically full circle. There is no end, I thought, and took
the first bus that came by. I started smoking for something to hold onto, no;
I started smoking because I need it more than you; no. I started because it's all ended.
    I'm out. What a drag. The man asked me for a filter tip so I gave him a full packet—
he said, *you sure?* I said *look, whatever.* I was drinking coffee and a guy came over
to ask if I was alright and I thought I was alright so I couldn't respond kindly. Life
was happening all around me. A blur, and a high rise, and the free fall no one pays to see.
    A blur—fishnets, made up despite losing, the loser, she
puts out those tentacles and is amazed to find the machete approach to rejection coming
from every attempt at soliciting affection. Bitch, you're no good. We say *should*
as in *should I jump?* or *should I have another?* Will you come? No, and no
and I told you so. The logical conclusion to everything is vulnerability
will get you laid, and if it gets you fucked over instead there's always obliteration—

how much is it worth? It's worth more than you ever earned in your life, darling;
if you want to see me drunk on your happiness, you'd better enjoy feeling the fractures—
    they won't be hidden, no. Run your fingers along them. I said, *run your fingers along them*.

Solar Plexus

You lean, and if someone takes you there is a compression of all wanted things
just under their skin and you cannot fit your hand into it. How many fingers
can I push inside you; there are bones either side, and I don't open easy. Today I passed
a blood clot and I wondered if something inside was more broken than I thought,
and when I looked at myself I saw my pale skin was paler and absorbing the shock
of being alone and more alone and more alone than I was when I was alone, even.

God, I'm subtle.
                        I placed my hand on your bare back, the sweat conjoining;
its acids ate at me; my own stomach ate itself to the point of pain that if turned to pleasure
would have bitten a hole in your side and woke an entire graveyard. I saw the doctor
who treated me in Costa; he glanced over, gently. I remembered him asking me why
I had no fixed abode. He had to pull my hospital gown up to feel my belly and told me to place
my hands by my sides and when I did the shirt came up over my breasts and I squirmed
as he kneaded into my tender cavities where the pain was busy soliciting—I thanked him.

And I'll find you, I said. I lay on the mezzanine floor and screamed myself inverse from delirium
and heard Katy tell someone *she's bottomed out*. I can't lean if you won't take my weight—
and I'm so glad you came, so hurt something. Here is a magazine you won't read, and here is a Kleenex,
and here is my phantasy of death, and you can take the felt pens and add to it; maybe a scourge,
a central shadow; perhaps a horizon I forgot to draw in, perhaps there was an ocean somewhere beyond
the peeling skin, the cannula flushed and the peaking morphine drip that made me think, somehow
I still was with you.

My Late Father's Decline as Sunset Fell Over the Sea

Dear Joe, I am being watched.
Your heart failed beside the ocean, I trace its persistent murmur here.
I'm afraid of the absence of language—
being held in the gaze of someone you want to see you
defies language—I mine for words—
your death stretches far beyond the view,
your view of the sea of your death, my view of the place where I'm living;
and I am alone all alone
though your eyes follow me
and do not close when mine close.
I blink at the black type on the white screen;
the cursor blinks back—my discussion with you develops
silently and is worked through as I edit out the flaws in my voice.
My voice a distant, solipsistic agent,
and I am positive the dead are bending my words.

Beyond my room, my desk, the sunset timidly holds us
in place—our house shifts all day
in between worlds. Father, I do notice. I walk out in the dry, cold air
with my greasy, boyish hair and
try not to limit my world to words as descriptions.
There has to be something beyond language, something there
and I don't know what or where it evolves and waits—
the sunset is a cloak and a curtain, and you close in.
You're where my silences hope to be reunited
with you in death, where every word
I neglected to speak is understood without my explaining,
where I close the eyes of the dead, and I kiss the eyes of the dead.
Don't touch me with your hyperborean hands,
wait for me to come. Everyone
has limits.

Come Back to Me

The asphyxiation was a whole winter in which I could breathe again.
And you won't read my solipsism anyway but if you did
you'd not need to slap me that hard to bring me round, I'd say when
to bail. But I don't want to come back. I'm untidying rooms
I'm not welcome in unless I breathe religiously or not at all.
And when you said *come back to me*, I did.

And this is addressed to my conduit for comfort and not the comfort itself
which invariably asks for back payment. I can't make money but I have temptings
each of which break the sound barrier with their squealing—don't dictator me—
to curl up on the floor hormonal and find the therapeutic harm in loneliness.
If you're not that lonely you shouldn't ask me to fill the hours
with my constitution for drink and taking punches

no bed is clean when I've deprived you of sleep in it; my sex drive is the last fall;
cold spots, a turning screw; and I break bedsprings with charisma and fall short of fulfilment
in excess. And I rub my wrists to check for a pulse that is stronger for having suffered
at the side of open mouths, bloated hearts and purring
a whole winter of blaming myself for having to lay here peeled
like Saint Bartholomew who did not want an afterlife when his skin burned.

Disappearing Incompletely

The cab driver told me about the *Art of War* and how in any life situation one must
leave an escape route. I said, *you're preaching to the choir, man*. I'm ready to cut and run
the second I enter a room. And I walk in, and I see you burn. The light is unavailable
so, I evaporate within the delusion that I remain unseen if I don't gaze back.

I lost my map. You told me you'd leave if I didn't know where I was going—
I left you there with your version of a city I belong in. This is *my* abyss. I love
to articulate things in my own way and have someone relay them back all bent out of shape.
He did something to you, didn't he? Yes. And you are experiencing overdue grief for a lot of sadness.

Well, I'd put it more like this: I haven't made my bed; I made a lot of beds, but not mine.
I left a lot of mess behind, but it was just detritus, it'll wash ashore—in the world I am escaping
through every door and every train carriage, I come home to no one, nothing and
you are somewhere else, not waiting for me; and I am not waiting. I am not.

Narcotise

But it's a trap; you pop the pill and hope no one notices the stoop. A white beluga whale
of pain relief and I swim, drunk in the stiffening grief and swaying, falling asleep
with my back to the world; and he lifts me and tells me to sleep. A junky once told me
the trick is not to fall in, to ride the high, and I stay with it, and even when my eyes roll
I'm conscious of everything. There's a gap between our lives and I
step over the crack and into pure soundlessness. This is
                                        the last line and every ending.

The numbness is a curtain that doesn't quite reach and so the light shapes me
into an inelegant star, once drawn, and the line fraying with my need to suck the life
out of your absence. Does anybody want to take me home, and she sucks it in
and pushes it down; the cleavage and the naked smile of me; you step in like a black marker—
the needle in and then you tell me about people who like to stick pins into their flesh for pleasure,
and you tell me the fantasy overwhelms and then it fails because reality.

Drink. The street corner is only fifty steps away.
I'll go under gracefully; don't you worry about me. I've been
to Limbo and Lust and I'm reaching Anger, and risen
like a serpentine failure again; around and around
I light it up and oh the air, and the big red burn, and the choking dawn.

Desperately

Morning comes desperately and we say *why don't you just take*
a Valium, like a normal person? Well, because the script ran out and postage
is obscene. I have shit to do anyway; you can't form a new heart
out of a fifth botched attempt at fashioning your own. God made sexual organs
sexy for a reason; and you can't run away if you already never
came back. I'll be un-fucked by NYE. You look basically like a vixen Goddess and I swear
I will basically look like Susan only uglier and yes, older than I actually am and obscenely
off-script in what can only be described as clothes too juvenile
for my own teenage daughter. Ho hum. I'll hold myself like a woman, it'll be fine.
I'm off the hanger now so it doesn't matter if I sprain my legs.
And anyway, who wouldn't leave me at the bar now; I have learned to smoke,
I guess. The fairy lights do full justice to a silenced love-of-echo; how I adore
blowing smoke over them holding my badly rolled cigarette with already chipped
£20 shellac nails. The patent whore-red is a smokescreen; dude, don't touch anything.
I was never a prostitute by the way, I didn't even *like* sex that much.
I didn't aspire to perfection, that's the thing; so, when I glow
it's because there is serendipity in a losing streak that wins out big in *experience*.
Have you ever been experienced sweet thing. You have now, darling. Take it, use it;
but you can't smoke this, or eat it; my oral fixation needed putting it check anyway
and what you take off you can always put back on you know—
you didn't think of that when you stood there naked with so many watching.
Denise Riley zipped me into my death's door red dress and I ripped it even before the show.
No one wants a torn manuscript but what about if I fill my mouth with text
or spit it out at your loveless face, or put the pieces back together in the wrong order, yes
that's sooooo darn experimental, isn't it? Oh, we're on such form, hanging out
in our ex-marital pyjamas, sucking the lobe of a slice of lemon cake; birdsong comes
so early as the year ends. I just wish the nights were not so endlessly *me* but perhaps still endless.

Nazi Soldiers Dream of Making My Day

Your life in my hands is a done deal—
    nurtured like a city in the mind of a King.
I don't want you but I bleed in your memory.
    You used the word fuck to describe what you wanted
too liberally—the waitress brings me a gingerbread latte and I wait
    for the best lover I ever had to come breezing in, he bleeds
all over Blackburn like a flogged martyr but he
    smiles patiently and sexily whether I like it or not
and like only an exceptional thirty-something lover can.
    Sometimes, I think, to write poetry you have to
not write poetry—
    I apply creamy lip gloss and spoon the froth into my mouth
I want him inside my body and you out on your ear—
    the further away you are the more rational I feel—
we're in bloom, and I crawl around looking for my veins.
    I'd text Bobby but I'm afraid of having nothing to say.
In my internal life I have a thousand children, all hungry
    and not enough arms to protect them from harm
—Nazi soldiers recall comrades smashing babies' bodies
against the sides of concentration camp trucks until they're silent
    and transgender scrabble champions take their own lives—
the callus where the pen rests on my index finger scrapes clean off
    and leaves a swollen, red lump
and there's a lump in my throat as I read The Guardian with him.
    I want him every minute of the day and yet struggle to orgasm;
it's an unfairness I feel is out of proportion
    with my incredibly compassionate realism. Just how immediate
can a poem be?

I am writing this but soon I will be typing this—
    erasing, editing, never pastiche, always influenced
by the splitting second rupturing each rational and spontaneous thought—
    the headline in my heart is: Do Lovers Ever Really Die?

An Annie Lennox song (not her best) plays on the radio in the pain clinic;
    the string section slightly retarded, as is the synth. 'Talk to me.'
And we sit here silent while I write this nonsense while
    Nazi soldiers in interviews say it was the worst time of their life
they never got over the slaughtered babies; their worlds
    fell apart. He reads *Lancashire Life* magazine, urges me to
hurry up with the novel, there's an £895,000 house with our name on.
    Poverty is not so unfunny these days; I eat the value range yet still
manage to look good in black. Poverty realises itself, even imagined poverty,
    only in lieu of the obscene wealth of others. Others often less talented
than my good self. Side-splittingly ridiculous figures
    attach themselves as captions over each necessary, concrete thing.
How can we save money today? How can we save each other?
    This morning my orgasm made me self-conscious
and he saw me stare at a young girl's behind but was I thinking
    about *wanting* her or *being* her, if only for a split-second.

Nazi soldiers dream of making my day and I cry—
    my nurse falls over herself and into the house scratching
her perfect thigh and hands me a prescription I have begged for
    since nine o five am, just as she was entering the building.
O Debbie give me back my ability to make witticisms and live
    without adequate sleep or dysphoria. How many babies
against the sides of trucks and how many times a triple letter score
    before the knock at the door is someone official. She had
pink hair and she was called Mikki. There are many sexualities
    all explored but not described in The Guardian on a Tuesday afternoon and
when I ask you I say, 'so if you had to shoot a child on its knees,
    or you would be shot or tortured horribly, or else
you could simply shoot yourself and eliminate the atrocity'
    you say you would shoot the Nazi soldier. I say I would shoot myself
but oh dear my darling as if this was news to you.

Imposters

        Awaiting despatch, I wake in time to see the sun set, and go out in a dressing gown and overcoat
to look more ridiculous and be unwitnessed. We are all, each of us, superfluous.
Out here, I dream of those I most want to come by; they won't. Locking me in means
taking me away. My chest bears down into my ribcage in pain because I want to be alone;
then being alone I want to be held close, then being held I dream of absence.
I dream of my absence. I dream of the absent. I bore myself—
being gazed at makes me feel sickened. Then I want to be gazed at when the gate is closed
and the traffic has died out in the distance; no one would need
to drive through this place to get somewhere else—you wouldn't come to Sparty Lea
unless you were a poet. You wouldn't come here
unless you were breaking, and at 1,920 metres above sea level, I know how to break.
                                                                                                                                Last week we rode
the train to London, stood
                    in the LRB where I geared up to have a tantrum; I was pre-menstrually
                    self-glorifying, and I turned my attention to Frank Stanford's hardbound Collected,
                    and the absence of his opus,
The Battlefield Where The Moon Says I Love You. And how predictable to want a thing that is not there.
The hideous child in the London Review of Books, the author of the pink slim volume
they say 'flies off the shelves', in her faux leather trousers, white t-shirt, braless,
and we walked to the place Žižek was spotted—dissatisfied with the coffee house he moved
to another across the block. John waved his arms and said *he's all platitudes* anyway.
When we covet, we detest the coveted object being infantilised, or being rejected, or being dismissed
by an apparent fraud. To find out that fraud is in every way as perfect and every bit as flawed as us.
So I choose one slice of gluten-free coconut and raspberry cake, eat more than my share
and John watches me reach my vice-laden Heaven whilst my nipples harden in the cold air.

London is grim to me when I'm waiting
at Notting Hill Gate after landing an agent
for a book I have not written yet, listening to
You Can't Always Get What You Want—
walking past a homeless man whose sign read obliviously
: 'do not give me money or food

I am an illegal immigrant,
a Romanian Jeepsy.'

Reassuringly Bourgeois

Sweetheart,
                you can't just fall into the sea. The pragmatics of destroying yourself are terribly complicated,
I live without a future and the hours just run into a kind of fizzing melee of endless transition.
I sunk a load of drinks and none of them really did it for me. You can't ingest food through your nasal passages
unless you're on a drip but everything I put into my mouth seems entirely discombobulating—
intense sensory overload and I spill over your limits and disconnect myself from the inner turmoil of
the relatively sane bourgeoisie. You don't know where you're going, but I won't get you there.

      I wish you'd make it easier for me. And then it's so easy for me I really wish I had to work harder
for a similar euphoric effect. My God, it's just too easy to exist, and the fact we have little choice in it makes it seem
a devastatingly uncomplicated lucid dream, but why didn't you dream it for me. Waking with night terrors I email you
and tell you I've gone insane. *You're not insane*. I knew you'd say that. *You're not alone*. You really think that. I steal
a chicken sandwich from Morrisons three minutes before closing and regret nothing other than this disabling
ineptitude to be with myself. Love mimics psychopathy;

you're hyper-unreactive but quite stunningly humane, you know darling you really can't eat cocaine.
Won't someone just buy me a boat? Some rich asshole with money to burn just buy me something to sail away in—
I get so far in a week it's like I'm eternally sinking. Well you know these things make you crazy baby
but do you really think you're madder than me? Look at you. Sure, you're nothing like the elephant-hugging
sedative-addled poet we once enjoyed the company of. You're in fact just an entire stratosphere
of incomprehensible data. Boiled down to an essential nucleus, you'd probably commit telekinetic murder

but I *desperately* want to stroke your face. *Everyone tries to kiss me*. It's a terrible burden to be so adored;
wouldn't it be lovely if everyone loved you and did things for you and when you really fell apart
they all just rallied round and made you feel like a worthwhile human being and stuffed ten-pound notes
into your knickers at regular intervals, wouldn't that make life better. Oh I do hope
some rich asshole comes soon and so I can get back to being a bourgeois sitcom version of me.
Oh I don't mind if you lie to yourself but do it with your mouth closed. In fact always close your mouth

when you speak. That's better.

I'm Amazed

Tramadol, UHT iced coffee and prosecco make me a more accessible person;
you think you'll get your money's worth with me, then the bill comes.

There is a bone lodged in the throat of my life. I didn't submit to this spanking for nothing.
If you can't give back my expended gratitude when I want it, don't ask

for a double helping of me. My face is about as breakable as your maxed-out afterlife.
Look at this mouth, does it look like a safe place to keep a fantasy.

On the Underground I wondered how I got on the train, couldn't remember
where I got on, thought, 'shit, I'm high again. Do other people cope as well as me

when they're this strung out in a capital city?' But it goes without saying you can't experience pride in relation
to abusing someone else's prescription medication. I didn't

pay for lunch. I forgot to pay and I gave my change to a homeless man in a neat
check shirt who told me about his rehab experience. He kept telling me

he wasn't drunk, whilst I stood there on the other side of a fence with a pint in my hand.
The bouncer vented his grievance at having to keep moving the adjustable fence

to various points plotted with brass dots the council had marked out for certain times of day.
We sat down and he carried our table away. Then he took the chairs. John was wasted

and couldn't understand why God had cheated us. A hot cokehead
described his job, with his dilated pupils and overstretched sensory perceptions.

He said a clause in a law made over one hundred years ago meant that rich people
could sue other rich people if their properties took up too much light. He said

there's an awful lot of money in it. We have a right to light, he said. We looked up
at the moon. Sweat ran down my thigh as his mate touched the tattoo on my lower back

really quite tenderly, though I hadn't given him permission, and he later said
I couldn't take a joke when he laughed about me being covered in roses. I'm also

doused in light, and I didn't get permission to soak in it. And who will pay the fine
when I absorb too much sunshine? The solicitor told me defence law was redundant.

He said it collapsed for him when he had to represent an eighty-four-year-old man
who had raped two generations of his own children. And fuck Hilary Clinton.

I walked the American back to Farringdon and we took English tea into the
empty breakfast room of the hotel. The concierge wouldn't let us sit

in an otherwise empty room. John said, what crazy fools we are
not to realise there is a separate empty space for breakfast. It's important we observe

the rules. There's no divine intervention for our seating needs, John.
This is just the world we're living in. Oh my golly, and Amen.

One Eye Open

Because I'm not tired, and should be sleeping. And there is no bed for me, and no door;
you're sleeping, you slept five times today whilst we sat around bored, you slept,
you sleep. I am in hotel rooms aching and drunk and not sleeping,
and in other people's beds, aching and drunk and not sleeping
and watching trains go by not sleeping, and watching them and thinking *this time*.
Because you cancelled me out. And the onus was on me,
so I took chances where I could just to create the idea of having a chance.
     I'm done,
and the catapult has lost its tension. I could go anywhere but here and still be nowhere.
I'm still nowhere whether I'm here or not and you sleep whilst I sit with a noose
contemplating my worthlessness, and you sleep, and don't think of me and I am not there,
and I am not here either, and I am out of options. There is no room. There is no I.

So I choose between self-preservation and self-immolation.
Not sleeping with you here, not in a bed with someone who sees me and grieves my leaving.
I pulled all the chicken off the bones so you would have lunch tomorrow
and I sucked the chicken off a small bone and glanced into the room you were in with our children
sleeping, them tucked around you like little obstacles; and they're not obstacles to you
because you have placed them here and there and scattered them around in comfort
and shown them I'm the one who leaves, and you're the one who wakes in the morning.

Appulse

Motion; yearning for. Separation becomes amenable after the rope frays and we sense the drop—
safer to stay hinged, no matter the pain of accepting it. And I play you songs you hate
in the car you spent all our savings on when I left; evacuation music; a tearless face—
but loss makes argument irrelevant. I am me now, and she, and all you never wanted,
and you hand me my bags and calculate the allowance I can take out our account;
won't even cover the cost of making it back. You reel me out there, I'm burning up.
One day I'll be so rich you won't be able to look at me and
you took a girl out this weekend and our kids asked where you'd gone.
I'll make a living if it means digging; the high point is the appulse—I get high all day and lie
in the bath twitching.
                I got this.
                            Elopement, grief, aching, below-freezing
I write about the opposite of lack-of-affect, I assume the position of posthumous
literary failure. A flaw, and you show me the door, and you will meet me there, because I'm danger;
deal with the chill, and then the nerve seizes up, and the veil comes down, and you ride it—
what I wouldn't give for the antidote for desire; or for the object of my desire, or for comfort,
I walk around in these sheer black stockings as though I've ever been looked at—
and then I come around, and the sound of your voice makes me violently hopeful; so shiver all night.
Incubus, where are you? I'm beyond cold. The grave has no air and no mercy, and no nightlife,
and no fun. You're maybe only an hour away from me,
                            and Christ, it smarts.

Whitechapel after rain & then the long plateau

still I can't imagine him asleep or you smoking a pipe or peeling an orange
but oh how my imagination persists with your violent suffering over me. An empty picture.
Me not in it. Let's do something. It's exciting me. Eyes scratched out with
lack of dope. I wanted to be held & if it involves rope, red pain and a collar I'll not only be there
I'll take pictures of it. *Just between you & me* is something I never heard before. But we laugh at murder,
and the missing schoolgirl from around the corner won't come back unharmed.
I woke up craving nicotine but like you I see eroticism in the desolate & unsated &
I don't smoke. It was a Lynch weekend but it moved quickly into Bergman.
Then Dick & I walked through Whitechapel where we gesticulated in half-hearted
drizzle and he said it was the kind of weather only a mother could love.
We could visit Henry he said & I inhaled hard and didn't hesitate to decline &
I came & on reflection, I told him, I think it was the cocaine.
Packets of pills all over my room and I've scrubbed you out of it
for the sake of the sanctity of Myself. Hot bruising & facial bites &
I have died heavily, almost sleeplessly, ten hours out of one hundred &
a thousand climaxes detonated submissively. It hurts more, yes now & I could tie you up. Right now yes &
cut into it if it doesn't hurt. Nothing can be undone that leaves marks like these.
Your belt around my neck and your hand pushed into my mouth. Tighter.
We all condensed into that in shame and pleasure. & you, too, have watched me bleed.
– Would you object to it. I'd die for it. You'd die. I'd kill you. Yes &
I'll kill you back. Will you. I want you to. Really. Please. Yes. I've not come inside you
because I don't want children. I ate your children just now. Yes &
I'm totally fucked. You did all those things yes but
you also wrote about it. So it's ok then. You write it down you're absolved from it.
Did you not know? That's why I'm so good—I create my own absolution
and win prizes for it. And someone on Twitter says I'm writing about
body objectification whilst you bite my breasts and I cry voicelessly.
Cokeheads wake up numb and I am bitten all apart.
I go down to the off licence and the shopkeeper tries to sell me eggs several times
when all I came for was obliteration. I delay so many things to feel them fully.
& yes Dick I'll show up in all my excruciating splendour for the leaching voyeurs
because I've got nothing. Even a masochist knows when they can't lose.
I accumulate bad decisions, my sugar coating helps

& that is all. You think you'll win this one? Well, I think I'm the only true fuckup there,
so wouldn't it be more of a show to give the money to the one
with the most bruises. You know. & yes in red I will hold my guts in &
bow, and get on my knees for you. If I could sleep right now I would but instead
I might neck liquid Prozac and swallow tramadol and try not to get too fucked at 5 A M.
I'm not proud of myself, if you were wondering. You can't take pride
in dying better than anyone. & yeah, when it comes it comes hard for me.
And my death will be a very wet orifice. And everyone will push into it
and enjoy me.

Mobile Slaughter Hall

I've imagined such proximity you have no idea—
what you need will harm you & I—the deliberate impulsively relieve of pain—&
I need my choices made for me. These lane conversations. Insects & drug dealers
in transient lambent. I chase a frog under a fence whilst kerb crawlers connect
with my inner violence and coast the cemetery for used baggies.
No one walks away from me—

from me & I don't speak. The senses honed and M shares the name
of the man I situate in the impeachable sovereignty
I can't devour a heart. He's so kind, M, I have to be cold.
Boys smacking each other in the name of balance. Smack &
you are not kind and you said it. You remember pethidine, its colours
and the flavour of doping & screwing. Salt, a lean mistake.

Your intimacy banes. I'll hollow your soul out with my tastebuds—
red & red lolly. We spoke of the sucking in. The absorption—bodies
rigid in the Ganges. What did you see. The inner child won't be murdered—
and again we block out the sound. She tickles your foot with her ankle.
No one knows us. You string me up by the ankles—
the blood rushes to my head oh God Christ Fuck how I want to replay.

The thread. All else buckling beneath it. So tightly it hangs.
And, again. The crook of your arm is the crook of mine—darling—
we have shared nought but blood between us—the clot curls into an embolism
danger into my mental space & we imagine un-death, a broken branch,
nothing holds the weight. I go blue over you. The vein shies under this light—
shit—this bright blue yelp of digital submission.

The pictures of you replay on a fascinated loop. Particular expressions
void gut-feelings. Dennis Hopper inhales—a lifetime beyond totalitarianism,
now we are just a mouth. No one else calls time on this room.
It's time to stop now. Stand back. There's no clock. Impatience can't walk—

snuff a teaspoonful of tequila—bedtime routine down—stringent the military
precision of your avoidance. But you lay back sant. The swab—

manufacture an absence for the terminally medicated. Grip. Snort &
there it is—your amnesia worsens at the sight of my bicep—
the blue trail of an addictive personality—the tangle of a golden shaft of indecision,
but that moment will come as long as you maintain the dam. & I walk down
to the abattoir. You know I like to be with the animals—pouring out,
executioned—the blood is hot. My clenching hands cook.

White cells hide the opiate. I just need to be fixated.
Tying the straps. We hold the wild & casual abeyance—you're mine—mine
but no sofa, sofa bed, bed, no wall, alley, nothing
to press my palms against. Blowjob hotel & you reach for your wallet
& two months later cash touches flesh. Thunder reaches—no backstop, the gun inert—
chest cavities crackling with phoenix-like abuses.

They crawled away—don't pull it, more will come. The hole is so tight &
yes so hot &—moonlight ditches—the holes cool the horror—concave
are the anxieties—the slaughterer shouting *Allez Allez*
and the hoofs maw—and I get so hard. Coronary bliss she finds a vein.
You shudder as she comes to. Objectifying every landscape, and she
and she has never seen you like this—so you could be anything.

It all makes such sense—pore, skin & muscle are the strapping-on
of God's favour over the medicine flush. & death is its intersection—
killing me—and the whores digress to look healthy in love—my best dress
shimmering cat's eyes—shows up the cellulite—the drugs look so pretty and secular.
Talking myself down—she misses it—train journeys; long comedown.
This is not high enough to kill you—the higher you get & the more the kill.

Sheets wet—the desperate interface between us and this hook—
unreliable narrator I don't want an imperfect lie. The jaw pumps and the fist

internalises. Nothing but a human in the core of that & I get white
on litigious dreamscapes. Masochism without opposition. Victims
call to cry themselves asleep whilst I deep-throat life.
Shush now—my breastplate yearns your lap—& the milk tastes good.

The cot creaks. We don't look at it.
There is no mood here by that name. No free stables to rest in nor
offices to organise your heartbreak. You signed it all away—
the stainless steel—the mass manufacture of it—& if
I counted up everything I stole when you were squatting—
because netherworlds have a points system and your reticence gnaws my sleep.

You disagree with a nod. Eyes closed. The approach is slow &
my restless torso—then collapse by—shot up like a Christmas morning—
& I can taste it—it comes—here—golden—little—wrists.
I feel angry about what he did, on your behalf. I really feel bad. Why did he.
I didn't do that, I fear having done it in a previous life. I'm mad, right?
But what binds us you don't see—it is only the bind itself—
—dead broke—that holds my need to thee.

Until The Last Light Goes Out I Was Still Here

Don't talk to me about discipline—I just stood outside smoking with no pants on
and I'm not even pissed. Out of sleepers, my insomnia is so rampant I've taken every
soporific drug left in the house just to engorge the next four hours so it fills the hole.
You want to look at me. You want to look at me. You look at me—I'm the last person
you want to look at. Trust me, it doesn't matter how far down you descend, when they say *spiral*
they mean *sheer drop*, and yes, when there's nowhere left to go you'll find a recess, you'll find
the back alley, or the bad dream, or the waiting room, or the black out; it's there;
you won't have to struggle far to reach it. There is no end. It goes on forever;
I dream of a house and every room is empty. I look for you—in a thousand and sixty-nine nights
I have not once sensed you there. Sometimes there is a broken chair, a falling curtain,
but no body, no bloodstream. I get wet thinking about the needle you're holding.

    You make a scale model of my life. There's the park bench, and the graveyard;
the people looking on; the jumpers; you haven't made me yet; you're worried I'll look different,
there's more I can lose; the pain is unquantifiable—it doesn't quite work as a 3D art-piece,
for all your efforts—you can't fashion clay into a realistic ghost. You can't bear to touch
the parts of me you'd have to fix.
    When you go, turn out the light for the last time.
I'll have to feel my way around the walls to find the switch. And I told her when the switch goes on
I can write it—but you know there is no switch. I say a lot of things for money and sex;
The pain is not palatable, I know; maybe if we re-model the book as a script and draft in
Michael Fassbender. Someone attractive in place of me; minus the scars—the scars could sell,
but then again, your readers think they want to see them, but they crave the smooth skin
those other writers wear for bed. So turn out the light; if I'm crying, just pretend you have
somewhere to be; yeah I know you're lying. Yeah I always know you are. Don't worry about it—
who would want to lie next to me? No one sleeps next to the ravine, do they? Or do they?
Oh, the junkies, yeah. Oh, and the molested. Oh, and the emotionally replete;
and no, these hundred beds I've died in this year didn't like me either; I left them so clean;
it was almost as if I didn't exist.

With Gun & Regret
for M

          On the street, the air doesn't circulate; 2 A M, dehydrated; I live with gun & regret—

                                      where are you and
everything breaks away into the dumb slow-drip of counting hours—was always
on my mind to last a week more then cut loose the damned leniency I grant myself as though
I am the perverted schoolmaster of my own weaknesses—you get an A grade for trying, girl
but seeing as you like to go so low;
                         you didn't find me, I just appeared, in black, in a silhouette
guarded, velvet, you walked up, I looked awful; sleek and awful, and you spoke, and I said something like
I had a new collection, you asked the title, I said Sunshine, I said something like *it's fucking miserable*
    made you laugh anyway, made you laugh and that laugh and we walked away

you woke me up

           then you don't come back—some things are just there—I'm just there, you're just
do up your laces; I bend over less, it's that constant pain in my uterus, like my body is saying stop this
and now my back is a cold, hard place you know, my grief breaks over everyone I intimidate with touch—
I looked at Keiran when he said he was trying really hard not to just fuck me and I said
there's a lot of pain in me, you know

                                  you used the word *fucking* in context, it was a joke but you saying
that word is not right, you're not that, you are not—you are not and you are not
I can walk into a room and locate you without seeing you even if I didn't know you were there
I swear.
        But I fastened it tight, too tight, it won't work—
relax a little now for me sweetheart—
        grip the stirrups—just a ride away, and into something feasible, I want that
I got a lot of mileage out of being the outer limit
all the temptations melt into a dream—my night is your night, you just don't know it
I'm feverish, constructed a party for my flatmate just to stop myself shaking
hands dried out from wringing and lungs packed in from smoking and body so tense from
doing nothing about the pain—just feel something more than what you were built for

                    Trouble is, when it goes cold you don't want it. Look at the plate,
all of it swimming with what should taste good and I rarely see you in daylight,
just at night, and at night I tell myself not to think about it. You, the things I want; then poets
and I sleep with a genuine Giacometti print; images of my children; images of the skin
I most want to touch, the skin, and what I want to touch, and how it's paper-thin, and how it suffers;
and I used to put out my hand as a child to touch things I couldn't reach—my hand reaching
never reaches.
            —I wish I were air,
a signifier, I wear my favourite clothes on days I hate myself most; lift me out of this—
lilac round the eyes, an inability to ruin my make-up by crying; where are you and
am I a great writer or just a fluke, or am I just a wreck, and why have I done this to you, again
and why do you hate me apologising for doing this when I can't help it you can't help me and
when I sleep I am no longer anywhere, and the world doesn't miss me.

Relentless misery has no real poise she just has so much to say to make up for the silences
my arm around my boy, his heartbeat; a candle lit next to a photograph of Steve who fucked me
after being my father for years, teaching me to paint, I used to visit and sit with the great man
at his black painted table, on his black painted chair, he'd show me his studio,
filled with empty whiskey bottles, no sunshine and no
he doesn't breathe now he's dead, I think.

                                    There's a lot of love in washing up, I tell a friend
and think of you. I understood so much of what you wrote, I saw how people admired you and didn't
hear it—made me want to pull their hair, pretty poets insulting each other by explaining themselves,
no explanation for us; try explaining you to someone who hasn't suffered.

Run aground, and I say
I'm in love with you I hoped it would peter out, read it back the next day, comedown
again, I'm so sorry I did that, it's not even funny, or sweet, or flattering, or cute—it's not wrong
but it's not right, and I held myself tight. Lip-bite, heartsting, leaching on my own impulses,
never trusted 'em, withdrawn and I will take the kids to the place Gilbert and George eat
every night at 7 PM, down the street, like they care and like

I care and
like I care and like I care and I care and I care

it's because you care you don't write

Battlespace

I saw someone get crucified. In the desert.
        Hold onto me. There's no need to say sorry, then you say
'you'll never in your life experience pain like this.' And then you look horrified and add
'and God I don't want you to. I swear to God I don't want you to.'

No instant relief. The shots cost £400 each, you can't use them too often. And
you fell into my chest and
                I put my arms around your shoulders and you sobbed, swore;
the pistol you keep on your chest is called Last Option. They taught us suicide.
You took your fingers to your chin, pushed your head back; looked up. You'd practised this.
If they come for you, if you're shot, you have to do Last Option or they're gonna do some fucked up shit to you
I mean so fucked up, you can't even imagine.

The cold snap got under my skin, and we dropped some Valium
I sat across from you at the table, sipping tea, eroding. You stank
of vodka, and I stank of cigarettes and you somehow managed to cook me an omelette—
a Michelin star saucier who did too many drugs and joined the army to get clean.
You know where I've been. More or less. You say I'm the pure finest.

        But the pregnant girl you saved, the four-hour standoff to stop fifteen men stoning her to death;
she'd gone out to buy corn, without permission, and spoke to a man who wasn't her husband.
You wanted to kill all of them. You would rather have killed or been killed than she be executed.
Madness does not describe any of this, there needs to be another word—
twenty times today you murmured *war is bad.*

A cage, the size of the studio flat; seven burned bodies, locked in and set alight.
Two babies lying on ten pounds of semtex.
A father blowing up his little girl as she stood there on the roadside crying in a bomb-jacket.
Dust. It was just a cloud of dust. It was just dust. I was just dust, and

you'll be able to come to a war hero's funeral. Twenty-four soldier gun salute. The Irish flag and the Union Jack
draped over my coffin. They give it to your partner. I haven't got one.
        The omelette was soft and warm and dripping in butter. The room you keep in darkness

and only go out at night. You hate the daylight. A black towel over the window in the front door.
No more of this. *I should've gone with my boys.* Shaking hands with Prince Charles.
You listed the names of your platoon who all died though you were somehow revived.

You said, I died.
I said, I died three times.
You shook my hand.

      Face down on the bed to straighten the spine whose vertebrae are dying.
I lay next to you and placed my hand on your shoulder, your grey vest, your wheeze, your
incomprehensible sentences. Can't see the sun in here. But you told me of the sunrises over Afghanistan
and I told you of the sunsets over India. But then

you told me who you'd murdered and why. You said they locked you up because
you had the psychological profile of a rogue killer. *Sarah, Sarah…*
Oh God. *I loved her to death. Five seconds. Pssst. Gone. Dead.*

Why am I not dead.
Why am I not dead. Why am I not.
Why am I not. Dead. Why. Why am I.
      There's no adequate response, I say. You lean against my breast and your spine shudders
and then you show me how you put the gun in his mouth. *Babies. He put his babies on enough semtex
to blow a two mile square radius. I put it in his mouth. No, I shot him in the leg first. Then I put it in his mouth.*

The first one, I vomited.
The second one, I had to pick up, half of him hanging off, to remove him.
The third one, I wanted to do it.
The fourth one, I was ready.
The fifth one. Barely felt a thing.
The ninth one. I loved it. I wanted to do it again.

      You described so many war crimes, many perpetrated by you, this afternoon,
high on morphine; you are not the only one, this is

worth crying over darling. And if I witness anything, I say I can take it. Don't worry,
I can take it, but tucking you in, and walking back into daylight, clutching myself,
lighting a smoke, walking—a howl
people driving and cycling—as though we dare to be consoled,
and do you know I was tortured
and do you know, no, I never told anyone.
You don't come back from it, and I keep my mouth shut.
No one gets to see it, no one ever could
      and I'm miles away from any war zone but
if you're a woman, in Afghanistan, you're fucked!
If you're a woman. And everything hurts—if I had *Last Option*
I would've used it by now. But I had this to do, darling, I had this to do, to fight
and no one told me to do it, and no one told me what was right
except that I must suffer, and bear it. And the day collapsed

sunset rolling around in the dust; pain in my chest like I keep my self there, bruised
by being so unwitnessed. I see you
and come in.

Duplicity: A Letter

Man I just love it when you push that needle into my vein and ask me how I'm doing and I faint and you
put the fan on and it blows over me and you elevate my legs and check my pulse and all that and then I open my eyes
and you look at my dilated pupils and give me water why can't all romantic interludes be thus.
   Don't faint. Ok. Just don't. We have to carry this shopping back my god you have this film of sweat again. *Chocolate milk, you're not ten*
You look pale, like you do when you get like this. You need to lie down again. You've slept for like the last three days. You know the weight
of what you carry most people couldn't. So sleep.
   Motionless, and I wait for
Line in. Head lolls. Pray for morphine. Make me well but do it with really high quality opiates please.
Does that hurt? Yes. This? Yes it does. Does it hurt when I press it here? Ouch.
Do you like pain? Yes. Do you like it a lot? No. I don't know. *Teethmarks.* I forget. I don't want to talk about it.
A really beautiful nurse just fucked me with a dildo it was obscene.
Being ill is insane. I haven't got septicaemia. But at least that wouldn't have been this boring.
   I bleed waiting. Two hours. Blood results. A little graph with lots of spikes. Frowning consultants. Bleeding from the biopsy site.
A lot of blood has collected, miss. You feel ill. Yes. You feel unwell. I do. I keep fainting. You're under stress. My hand on your chest. Is anyone there?
Stress, yes. Do you want to hear about my life? No.
Well it was entirely hell. I don't care. *Undress.*

Things you can't say to a doctor include
oh God I love it when you talk dirty to me when they say your breast feels hot and hard
you can't even say 'I've been waiting for a man like you my whole life' when they offer you
more exciting painkillers. There's a lot of cocaine in your urine. Did you know that? *No.*
There's blood in your piss. Yes. Does it hurt when I press this? God yes. More yes.
You're a little bit of a mess. Scars there and there and there, under your right breast. False tooth. *Someone knocked it out.*
Have you got eyes? I mean, have you?
   Makes me sad to think of myself. What makes you sad? It makes me sad when

   and Katy asked me what happened to my house when I was living alone with a baby
aged seventeen and I painted all this abandoned furniture all white I painted pink roses on the chairs
and I painted the floors got high on the fumes and I painted the walls oh it was so gorgeous I was so proud
I wish you'd seen it. Why does no one look. The sun melted over our worlds-apart day—
I felt I was with you but I wasn't anyway.
   What happened to all your stuff?
   Oh, that's a sad story.

He was the first boyfriend I had after all the rapes. He came in one day. He used to steal my money.
He smashed everything in my house to bits and cut the phone lines and beat me.
Blood covered, in a black satin nightdress. Clutching a cigarette with a raw shaking hand.

There is no poetry in this forgive me.
Was she beautiful? No. Does it still hurt? Do you take the contraceptive pill? Can we do a HIV test? Yes. Do you use intravenous drugs?
Not in years. *And the hiss god the hiss the hiss the hiss* Really?

Hopeless. Best lipstick on for the hospital. *Touch of amber.* Best eyeliner, all smeared. Try not to cry when no one's there. Lie shaking,
like someone in shock. Text M.   I just hope
sometimes it's *really I want one good thing to come* over with soon. Chest pains. Enlarged heart from all the poetics. You think I'm dramatic,
it's not nearly dramatic enough sweetness. Slumping to the floor of the balcony saying to myself 'oh for God's sake not again.' Trying
not to knock over the flowerpots.

Superego, you punch dirty. So why did all those men hurt you?
Because they were a bunch of cunts.
So, but why? So what did you do?
I was pretty, I had amazing tits. I never wore a bra.
I was homeless. I used a lot of drugs. I stole everything I owned. Intravenously. A nuisance.

And in my swarming recollections Jack Underwood offers me money just as someone hands me back my bag of cocaine sniffing
he withdraws his hand with deft reflexes and my reputation is shit in this town
we're a huge fan of yours I hate everyone in London for being able to afford their proclivities.
I describe my drug use to Luke as a 'far more desolate experience' being that I'm poor
and have always been poor. Sad face. *You're a celebrity now aren't you?* My inbox sobs with *I'm a disabled man so I can't come to you
but if you come to Hammersmith I love nothing more than to lick a nice clit yummmm*

It's all over now baby blue your body looks like something that should be in a working-class morgue
I guess there's a whole other demographic for that kind of thing.
                    I charge £100 an hour if I discern you can only pay that,
but I don't tell you that. If you are an arrogant piece of shit I will charge you a hell of a lot more
but I won't tell you that either.

And I was lovely once.
                      Tell me I was.
                                      You keep this much down your body starts to yelp and then it starts to
squeal and *bleed, cry* eventually it starts to alleviate itself of you. Something will fill the space.
                      You can't say you're surprised really, can you. Something will. And push it down as far as
No, but I am surprised. Don't be disappointed in me. Please don't be.
Words will fill it. Words fill space. That space there and this one here I'll fill—
                                  Because I just want to grab someone's hand in the supermarket and ask them to take me home.
                    And I sleep with a toy owl and Darwin-esque claws. I have no sensation between my legs. I spend money I don't have
                        getting my nails done because it makes me feel less of an animal *please take me* and more *home* like one of them
and I hate *I can't do this*
we don't want you to do this to yourself babe you only do this to yourself you can't see that it breaks my heart babe it does
                        titillate titillate titillate yawn
do you know what pleasure is? Yes
sob sob then what is it *it's the only thing I know*
it's when someone can't see you *you know pain too*
and then sees you *he sees*
and sees you *it merges, we merge*
and looks at you *he sees less when you need him to*
not at the intense black murk you have in your
and then they don't take anything from you
not even the horror
or the pain
I've seen and I can't stop looking
they just
sit you in their lap *let me look*
and have no idea what to do with you

do they touch you
of course they do
of course they fucking do
everyone wants to be touched
I haven't touched anyone as me for so long I have forgotten

it's all gone
is it all gone *please*
>	*imagine how well I can beg if I have to*
I can and
>	*I love you so bad it wears me the fuck out*

but why is your grief so related to all this sex and death
you have autonomy your autonomy is your writing and your mortality
you have a body and you are mortal and you haven't felt anything for six months
you haven't really felt anything not even that penis not even that kiss you haven't allowed yourself to feel anything
you have to allow and receive you can't just accept you have to give and take but you allow the harm in with no feeling
you're worth more than this you should see the doctor
>	*if only music was your drug*

Is it so wrong to want not to *I'm sorry you're in pain* hurt. *I'm not irrelevant.*
>	I write to bear being this person. *Indescribable, pangs* I've got a cocktail gown for Tuesday's event
black and slick like a human eclipse I have forgotten how to do it sober *would a little score hurt right now*
I suffer, and who cares clean you want to sweep me off my feet clean then perhaps if you wait another month
I'll be gone anyway *I want to be this*
we all wait a long time *laid there in the next room internalising your heartbeat*
are you dead yet yearn *I'm sick I want to be this girl I want to be this blood filled*
thing you love waiting— I forage in the hospital. I still always look for syringes when a nurse leaves the room
I have a bit of a kleptomaniac habit again *like a paw in a honeypot*
rabid drain the bad feelings can't you you don't change that much *get them out! Inject, repent*
you were so close to me I thought I'd die
>	well if I had always had what I wanted I wouldn't do these things *I'd take any amount of physical pain*
would I   *would you* I just balk when someone pulls me up on my behaviour *over this*
like who the hell *you look so great in that blue suit my god* gets to tell me what I can't do in this shitty life
a police officer saying I destroyed the evidence *you telling me you wouldn't wash that off*
do you know that when someone rapes you violently it stings
they keep the tapes
it's so swollen really it is
>	*you have an incredible waist*

       you have an incredible
       oh god it's incredible
       yes it's incredible
the semen will sting it feels like Satan has filled you with a thousand years of incest
I have a millennium's supply of divinity
   it's all for you
     I've got what you need I have it
daily beatings if you'd been fifteen he'd have gone down for the rest of his years I don't beg for mercy
attempted murder, multiple counts of rape and torture. The baby's his. Take it away.
Mercy must be granted independently *But it'll be years in the courts and you'll get dragged through it, unsupported*
I fell down the stairs but I was high on smack I didn't feel anything
I only felt it afterwards in intensive care and someone died next to me I felt it
I felt him dying I feel you dying living I feel you I feel you all the time you feel it don't you
   don't wear anything revealing
it's relaxing I can't wear that dress it's all cleavage the cleavage years are gone the drug years too the years all of them
be called as a witness, you'll have to detail five accurate accounts
over and over
I never begged I only beg for what I want
and if they're too clear they'll say you lied
and if they're too variable they'll say you lied
where's your mother

    why must I love anything
at all *even you live in another realm*

   and if I only love you until the end of my days I don't mind
   because I was never loved *if we are constructs*
   what does it matter I'd rather be a fantasy than nothing so I don't need love back
   honest *I'm not nothing I am*

a miracle

    she does a great line in evening gowns

I know you read it then you don't say anything I am only a heap of words I want to be a heap of words ceaseless
she is an incredible poet
she damn near killed me with that book *I'm sorry babe, that sounds tough*
you know I love you I loved that book, did you
everyone loves that book, right? *Do I have to be dead before someone cries about the suffering I'm in*
She is really kind. *Her breasts look joyous. She makes me laugh*
you know she isn't half as good as you I don't love her
she's really not
I love her
no I don't mind don't apologise keep being my fantasy version please I get so bored out my mind you make me vigorous
       rigorous I mean rigorous just imagine the epitaph, great commission
everyone does love you
I get a phantom drug taste down the back of my nose all day it kills me I erode

       the night is a constantly vacant thing my mind explodes with it a version of it not the real thing
the night is not real it is an idea it makes me want to break my head
I collapse now because I should've collapsed then and I didn't the fool is the one who doesn't break when they can
and I didn't for the love of god can't you see I should not have gone on it's a far out place you keep me
       I keep going—of course I will, for you
London keeps my babies in a sterile glass jar so far

Yes I married him and have no idea who he is *the tumour is sunshine filled*
       I'm serious and he has no idea who I am either he just wishes I'd vanish

for no real reason I cried on camera one day you'll see it it'll be awful a suicide letter I was so good at those
more sympathisers than I can work with on a daily basis but no real
I adore you
I really do
       I wish the world ill
but not you love
I wish you would hover over my bed while I sleep your hips aligned with mine not touching
or maybe touching, no always touching, touching like a silent movie, no not silent, I want the full of it
and then kiss me on the lips, I'm very primed but broken up you can't fix it but you can console

so that my body remembers but I never will
my wants are childish
and don't go away
      is what I said
regretfully yours

and I'm scared
and the grave is not a place you can sleep with me and I don't want to be there alone
yes it's that bad
yes it is and it is what if I wear my best dress surely you'll remember which my favourite dress is I point it out daily
I can make you laugh though the days are constantly vacant things I fill them with smoke and praying
      prayers are easier than hope or doping

She once sat in an Italian restaurant
      it's an impasse, I suppose
for seven hours ordering nothing but the cheapest wine

snorting coke in the bathroom playing with the stem of the glass stroking
atrophying flirting with the waiters delighting a selfie can't you involve yourself fatally
having an excellent time and good at it
the whole world went away like a neuroscientific discovery disproved
and you said *I bet*
      and you love me because I am a lyric poet I bet and that's it I say it like you want
and I only started crying at midnight
when there was nothing left but a slowly evaporating taste for the illusory object, objects, you

      She told me to tell you
      Allegorically   She said only nice things
      She was misunderstood   kind, she gave to the poor because she was *vultures*
circle because my heart radiates a sonic pang only you can
come, baby give it what it wants or just a heartful of it empty the day the night I need
more, now
She

Heroin

My friend, some desolation is so self-explanatory you are doing a disservice to language to describe it. And mine was
riddled up to the neckline in sweat-rimmed Viognier, post-editorial meeting, sinus-suicide cocaine, summoning the will to go home and sleep
as people do every day so I've heard; instead
                                              you see I knew what was coming so I met it on the incline. Some weeks I can actually taste the pain before it arrives—
my heroin addiction is economically viable and actually quite banal, which seems a shame. As far as rituals go it's just so perfect I'm sorry to say—
dealers take longer about it, and I realised last week I have no sense of time whatsoever, never think of it until I'm waiting to score down an alleyway.

Seconds blur to a halt in reverse. Some days I lie in bed purring. I lie uncomfortably and can't be bothered to move. The itching doesn't bother me; my whole body
infested with histamines and bliss; and I scratch myself for hours, and talk myself out of the value of intellect. Or Love, or liberty.
Never so enslaved as to this drug. Writhing all the way to Euston, back twinges, shakes, sweat and orangina. Is it realistic

to want to suffer less. I don't screw grandmothers over. I think up a reality TV show in which I train dealers to be better at their job;
food that is not even food sustains nonetheless; if I smoke it my lungs will forgive me in time for my shortness of breath I watch comedy shows with my eyes
closed and the world is on hold so tomorrow I will eat ice cream if I have to eat. That'll sort it. Yes.

Celebrated poet my arse. One breast and a desire to elope with the first person who loves me slightly more than their cat or their more 'stable' spouse.
I watch the sun rise and sun set as a counterpoint to how much do I need to set me right. My managerial life decisions make the ebbs easier to overlook.
Fuck's sake I thought I'd outrun the smack. Too honest to be really good at it. And that first hit will never cease to weaken me at the knees.

No you'll never live up to it. You know the cons but do you know the pros?
Heroin is the best lover I ever had and he doesn't even care if I drool. He doesn't care if I vomit. He thinks being incapacitated
is elegant. I apply red lipstick at regular intervals life darkens to a wound that ever fills with pus. They're saying

I'll live. Mouth around the tube. Never had reason to buy candles or cotton floss. I wish I'd never seen anything better than this.
I wish I didn't sit around stoned watching the better things exist; you have no right
to happiness. I wish you had any idea. No, I have no real home and I'm fine.

Monsieur.
I have no answer.
My veins plead for the sanctity in I no longer give a fuck.

Heroin II

A life bereft of 3 AM birdsong would be a tyranny of sunless misery. When the sun comes up it's all done and you are there now
fevering with me, and beside me I have a sense of selfless self that was kept back in the stalls with a raging boner for a life-that-could-be
no-longer-excruciating. I breathe lightly, a rattle of falling in, and now no deeper to fall we sit in a manky beer garden slugging an eyeful of each other;
and how I want to drink it and swallow it. It comes only ever so rarely, a true huge feeling of *all of this*.

I'd get into a chasm without you to heave ho with my nighttime; goes on forever love, no off-switch with me, and you climb on
and don't hold back from falling in. I get revved up, but it's the filling of all the hollow I most want, you are the exact opposite
of endless grief. No, I don't overshoot. My life was its own hovel, now we have the flowering of lights and sheepskeins. Trouble,
the green juice, and the rattle, the gallon of water it takes to get you through a seventy-two hour hell. I wrap up in a red wool blanket,

your cock asleep in its warmest sleeping memory of purring and hardening. The holiday heroin gave me was dreamscapingly gun-smitten,
but I want to come home. How much guts it takes to bite down on that inevitable drill. I want to go down
and you will enter the phase in which no one initiates your bloodstream to come up besides this fuck-up. Let me
trouble you more. I bring the things you most enjoy, and we picnic on the bed of our settling into the brave new sense of time, like unclucking insomniacs.

Get the red pen out, darling. I never said I could perfect any of it. I opened my mouth to speak when I was speechless at fourteen
and wished only that you existed. Piece yourself, uncannily. I need all of you in my wound and when the healing begins the future flashbacks will corroborate
finally finding hope. And what pain. And what destruction. Erasure of the time that wanted to hurt. I'll peel it back
suck on it with my new clean idiom.
                                    Be in your new limbs from Sunday, I come back hungrier, and suck; venom
I spit down the drain. Nothing turns black. The day turns on our faltering spindle; a cure, and nocturnal we unwrap the most precious wanted thing; powderless.
Substance in the form of sibling *wow* and a lick worthy of rapture. O I applaud what you've done to me. Sweetheart, I
live. Consciousness will rave with or without us; be in it and consent to riding it—ally, and zero dark.

Letter: 'too lengthy a prose for such a bad one' 4th June 2017
for M.C.

Woebegone to be readier than this for a flood; I supply myself with so much anesthetising experience, and sleep with one leg over the covers, bleeding, the wait and a red, foliage-shaped stain, sink what I can before sleep not to recall the impending dream of being blotted. Shut out in the cold in my cream peep-toe ballet pumps three-hour development of another humour; holding my wee in whilst the freeze-brain cringes, huffing, the street walking homeless approaching for acknowledgement but I see myself from the adjoining street and cry for her. The knock-knee Inferno of walking through the night with bloody feet; my Matthew I was tremendously afraid. Blood in my dress; faultless, true as only you see, and regressing right past 1993 —

      does it eat into your heart yet?
                                          White halter neck I check for bloodstains on the breast at regular intervals. Clutched the mic and elucidated Duplicity in a voice of several registers, to a room of housewives, hipsters, drunks and criminals. The men wept. Niall hung his head and couldn't look. I was praised, sweated, ducked under the outstretched arms of filthy-smelling sycophants. I have beautiful legs. I love your blue roses. Dressings, sanitary pads, sexual frustrations, *you are so wet I can't believe how wild you are I had no idea* all of it making me sick. Rohypnol in The Shakespeare, a Leeds United fan telling me, 'most girls are asleep by now; never had to give anyone so much'. It ate into my heart, but my heart spat it out into the street, and a

trio of horns played me out as the policeman put the red battering ram back into the boot of his car and drove back to the tragedy afloat on London Bridge. I escaped back through the hole in the weekend. It was quite tiny and I had to cut away some of the dross. I need a white dog to guide me through Hackney. I need a blindspot and a more refined spatial awareness that eradicates the need to blink. If you ring the police again they'll offer him a shrink. I get paralysed. The fullness of intent is often spiritless; if I could give you God I'd make him wear Yves St Laurent. A £10 bottle of perfume making my dress smell fragrant when it really should remind me of assault. The skin only wants succour, I lean out to you, throat-first.   Continuity of vision

      at the very least has given me a path
                                  the over-surge of hope leaves me tipping over in the bed-of-amnesiac-desires
haven't gloated since I humiliated David Harsent. Most existential complexity cannot be described, and nuance is so tactically avoided by the motives of simplistic bedfellows; enemies are often bored by my lack of investment in their hatred. I first understand I love when I realise I could spoil for a fight on behalf of that person when I know I couldn't win. My love is suicidally unhinged by a desire to defy it. How I would love you to put me to bed now; stroke my inner and outer and under-thigh, stroke until your fingertips prickle with there never being enough of us to fill the complete lack of opposition; I side with you, now

and the moment never fails to evolve into a spectacle, you know that in my head I have locked the frame around you and its fixed lock-down centralises an Adoration. I'm less polluted, but more strung out. My finger is on your upper lip, it tastes of me. I want your tongue and a riverboat expressly permitted to take me somewhere away from my poetry has eloped our poetries has stolen my notebooks and torn out the notes — Port now, and a guilty mind of dark orgasm and the sun lighting a wound that is made of bad bad men and my Mother digs her sucker in and you at least know it's alright to love like I love when I *get through them, get soaked, turn blue but get on the inward curl and Hokusai out of there*

Overshot

You can't blame poetry for this shit you're in darling.
What's poetry ever done to you?
      Did it wrap its hands around your throat at the point of climax?
Suffocate you with a pillow? Nope. Just lie down, and take it some more
like someone who can endure.

Are you irreversibly angry?
Do I reverse a month, two months, three years to make it alright?
I can't go out, can't
trust myself to lean against something harder than me

feeling of loneliness with name-calling and a tightly bunched fist to the mouth—
don't be silly now. It's alright. You just have to keep feeling; if you keep feeling it
it can't hurt overwhelmingly, there'll just be a pretty much constant feeling of hurt,
better than a blow, or several blows. Come on, count your blessings, chicken.

What did you lose? Your shoes, your favourite top, your money, your drugs, your
children, your children, your family, your children, your sanity, your home, your family
your health, your work, your agent, your sense of ever having limits, your courage, your pride
your love, yourself.
      You lost yourself. Go outside,
she may be still hanging out in the bar, trying not to die badly and badly
I have still managed to sink it all and look! It's all floating out there in a fever of defiance
because even as I lay dying I still wrote to you.

This System Of Values Has No Get-Out Clause

Everything with its equivalent medicinal weight and value. My body with its toe tag
wriggles in a stupor of complicity as I sleep numbed from these
hyper-ignorant self-preserving get-out clauses. Wrapped in so much floss I can't wake, and then
he calls because she's gone now and he can. My body isn't saleable anymore, it's
not deluded about how it presents; disappointing toxicology reports cannot be tampered with,
love; I dispute all things *thyself* then desire comes back to taunt me. No more,
and I'm waiting for you O Negative again. Chances come, you rebuke them.
You wanna see *my* work emails. They'll curl your hair and give you an impressive aneurysm.
No one is supposed to know what's good for them, that's not how ethics works—
O chaos. You get so exhausted bingeing on that stuff. Prolix.
                        I polluted it, so I have to clean it.
Twelve puncture marks and a string of bloody correspondences—a hole here becomes
just a hole all over. These toxic compounds are better for you than all the others. You take the
percentage and work with it. Statistically, you're already dead, I'm afraid.

You know that when you tell someone they're going to be fine it's to make yourself feel safer.
Honey can I soothe the very fibres of your despairing? A tickly cough, I fall in weak love, cougar, like—
I brought it on myself; I do admire you for it. I admire you for having the sense to recoil
from my sickbay deteriorations. And I destroyed myself in quarantine to prevent feeling exactly this—
I'm so sorry your girlfriend is nowhere near as interesting as me, but there's nothing I can do
about that. Maybe when she finally falls asleep we do connect.
My astral plane is well freakier than yours so don't count on it.

Is the blood red, black, thin or weird? Is it really happening and do you know my name.
Keep talking to me. M. Do it again. Dare me. I've never once flinched from pain.
If you google me you'll find my edifying nipples somewhere.
You daren't touch me but attempt to ruffle my hair.
Romantically overstepping is a promise of lollipops to a woman old enough to have given up suckling.
                        I will love you, and get me a wheelchair;
how dead would I need to be before it was noticeable. Spray tan me for the coffin;
darkest shade, streaks; properly fabulous is what you wrote me as though the fewer words you say
the more I'll go on. Lack accounts for every fight won. Knock the affection on the head
before it gets ugly like it gets ugly when mute swans raise children in dirty park ponds. You know

you want to, and choose a pink ribbon for the bouquet, maybe. My name emblazoned in gold.
Not because I'd like that, but you'll feel better. I care about you all feeling better as a solitary ambition; and I will
buy you a feral cat for the infestation—hope the pests all suffocate being toyed with. It's not liberating
to die happy. Whoever indoctrinated that idea was nuts. There are different kinds of crazy, anyway;
I'm the fun kind. *You seem fun*. I seem fun therefore I am.

        You look a bit lost.
I put my arms around you, babe, at the airport in Jaipur and my heart tapped out. Three days
and the worst is over; but then you are left with no excuse to go back. I think
I'm addicted to you. Maybe you think that and so I think it too. Maybe neither of us cares, and abstinence
does nothing for my nymphomaniac tendencies. You have to laugh because Elliott Smith
topped himself in a different continent under nuanced circumstances. I don't want to be erased so I keep
my rolled banknote. Who imagined the new plastic fiver could be so useful as an object. Don't
fuck it, feasibly complicated & hyper-consciously delinquent starfucker,
ever again.

Indelible, and Surely There

Surely there's time.
I think I have forgotten loneliness, deterred it, deferred the indelible thumbprint of it.
The dread on waking is now just named sunrise, or mid-afternoon sometimes, I am your new sleep.
And I gorge on the voluptuousness of disliking a new layer of flesh, formed virtually overnight by beginning to eat
and feel pleasure. Pleasure is not cold or cold-hearted. Whatever you say you stand a palaeontology of shut-down but ache; Jimmy hitting you
round the head, it's not you; your drumhead, re-scalped, unborn, and. No, they can't hurt what they can't reach.
                                                                            I dreamt seven yellow suns appearing
a last day and a last act. *Yellow ships, yellow kisses.* A puma and a snake in our room eating it. Heroin smoked, and the smoke tasting like
it tasted. A crackle of bacofoil and the tar-zip. Chasing the grey wisps, my burnt agent. You imagine my problems smote, settle in the river, we go to sea-hunt
—terrified, please don't leave.

My satin feels tight. My neck insists on cutting. I see London as a dead, blue whale stinking of the place.
My body-of-ribbon. Every single assault the last and never the last. How did I become broken by appealing to survival somewhere;
was there nowhere to go or did I want that to be true. I needed to be cornered and fight my way out, never thought
it'd be clean. My abdomen hardening, and I hate myself all consonants reading that poem; salt tongues touching themselves,
the devil and salt-nipples. Catch my breath in time to rise.

Surely. You are dreaming right now. Coffee on the melt; mending a vessel of words—words in the cot, tranced.
I look beyond, not above; *deep*. What is there to understand.
                                                          Most abuses are offered at the front gate.
I make them tea politely. I shrug when they call me a *cunt*. You touch your own hair and face. Ears blocked like sea-full caves;
can't hear or listen. Beacon of you, dying till it settles against the drums. You settle against my ass; describe my desire and it's close to pain
but fuller. Too big, yes, and whole-full like enviable unrelent. I ruin myself on vice and skip the antidote. Yes, I missed you.

    I'm not sure I won't get lost.
    Breadcrumbs, stones or sonar won't find me. I go.
    I'll leave it all behind for you. What do the departed miss, and do they look for you.
        I go to settle a score. Ask for more lime at the bar. Begin sentences, *sweetheart...*
        suck on that bitter juice and tell me what's wrong with this picture.

        If you return once, you know what it is to return. There's time.
I'm unswayably yours. Your love is not fictitious.
Riding wave into newness into a sky of storm, tornado fuzz above the belly-button, wet-licking your life to a menagerie.

Coffee circumcising the new Sunday. The regrets of a widow but no dead spouse.
I was tortured and your facial muscles won't bear it. So I thank God for what hurts and that it does,
and darling I

Solar Cycle Twenty-Four

      She wrote,
asleep in the benign and serendipitous arms of Bonnie Prince Billy's deserted voice—
hymns; so much to leave behind, and none of it lives in this mimesis. None of it thinks anything of vice
or basic affection. Vice as affection—sing this for me, asleep. To the tune of *Gulf Shores* or
You Will Miss Me... How I hold you in me, and you are the jolt of a record, and the echo of a feeling,
you said my book was all the feelings ever felt but my sense of structure fails with my body
as its flaws live up to my preceding reputation. It's important to decay—
I've got a bassline when I write; I have gyration and poise—recover, please, punk-ass bitch,
I thought of you playing venues with the stars I would have drink out of my hands
in a drought. But no one's thirsty now. Not even me—my milkshake
brings all the boys to the yard, or something.
            It's so hard to write into my visceral
farsightedness; I don't need a challenge, you are enough. Not free, you said; I said, it's okay. Leaving
is easier for me than chasing. I said I wouldn't be weird and you said well mostly people don't
need to say that and aren't, but gravity, sweet thing, *gravity*—we play hard because the only way to catch the ball
is after it's been thrown your way. I don't let go easy. I run towards so many ordeals
expecting them to move out of the way; I'll get nothing past you. Might as well
starve on the premise of being fed than within the illusion of starving.

Sometimes something is so good it can't be bettered.
              A hit; and the sun shines through
the sunflower blind; my kitchen is your chateau lobby—too drunk to read my poem, my prostitution,
how could anyone learn to live within a solicitude this palatial? Joaquin Phoenix my ideal bad lover.
I've been Deneuve and I've been Brando, and I've been Bardot, and I've been De Niro—
I do the bow and the curtain call so graciously when I'm the actress and the scene
begs to dig its nails into my tattooed back. Yes, darlings, you all have your name on the extras list,
but none of you get in unless you move me; and I mean *move*.

The girl teaches you how to be Humbert's demise if she knows what's best for a man.
I pull my socks up and roll with the diurnal skies. Flying and running into the twisting days—
somersault my hinterland, and there's more than one tie to bind, my love. I steal because I need power
and no one follows after me if I carry my weight. Shipbuilder, the hull of the boat
is an astronomical superstructure and you used your own hands to make the ark—want to touch them;

detonating; I'm anything to you and I can't pretend any more than I can swim over right now.
To drown; oh God how the wet clothes pull me down, the swathes, nothing feels the same,
and nothing is real to me, only my voice; it only responds to the dead in the shallows.
                              Inside, there's a picture show and a naked spread; deliverance is a wildchild.
Get your ticket and come sit by me and watch her in her foil dress making breakfast.
My dream is to never dress appropriately and go without a name. I should've been a star;
I'd have made it big with the right man behind me. Poke me in the turning side when I go bad,
and make me cry because I need to feel agony to know where the New Age tethers me. Ritualise
the first light and make it mine—you don't need to be here; it's enough to walk the line, but down there,
when you curl your toes over the edge, there is no abyss—just nod to me, and jump in,
the silence of us would never be pacifistic.

My mother once wrote to me to tell me *all the ways in which you broke my heart.*
I imagine it completed a circular void in her belly—light linking to light into darkness and I went
and came up to see her knitting a bad eighties jumper covered in geometric roses.
I don't know where this goes. Where do you want to go? Where do you want me? One hand
on the parapet and the other in my knickers. You could make me go blind. And the song
fades out to violence. An hour passes and Tim calls me up about this book and I consider the girl who wanted to be
anally fucked and cut on her wedding day.
It's like living in a Lars Von Trier film, only I'm less real. I made this for your pneuma.
       It's crazy to write to you. You make less mistakes when you're thoughtless.
I sip up my cherry cola and bite a kiwi fruit. The meaning never escapes me even at the foot of the hill
heading back through Dalston with my hands in my pockets, listening to my phone ring
but not answering. I guess you write better if you get laid, someone said. And the guy on the bus
says Chaka Khan is obese now. And the girl on the tube looks at my stupor and cracks open
her book, its spine can't take all this frantic wishing for the Motherland anywhere else.
                              There is a *Spiderland* for you of these arias—
I'm sorry there's always more. I'm your Jericho and you un-blind me. Post-rock bliss-out
but we knew twenty-minute tracks wouldn't stick. I do a couple of lunges on a park bench down
near Clissold Park, no smoke in my lungs; trying to kick and making a hash of it. My
baby was in my tummy when Sigur Ros played and the feedback made me vomit. I miss the kicks and how they felt.
Even the placenta dies. Baby, even the eyes blacken as the waves come down and over.

A reverse cowgirl and a reading of my palm. I blush as the volume goes up—
my tattooist tried to convince me to have my clit pierced last March. Last time I sucked a guy off
his silver cock piercing came off in my mouth and I almost swallowed it. Someone on Facebook says
you're such a rock star. Ew. Someone says *you have such presence*. I'm too easily accessed and I play up
to the image too much to be able to sit here in my old man cardigan typing with one finger
and eating ice cream with my other hand. I think about crucifixion too often. I'd sell more books dead,
but the glory would be given back to my antagonists. Oh, my boys, even you can't save me.
      When they take my picture
we'll live forever, won't we? My nude image will only invite more nocturnal messages
from laser-hearted poets who want a bit of fantasy action. I take a deep breath and turn towards you.
Look at the camera now. Look at the rafters. Are there any angels out there who understand the math
of this? Sure, baby, but nine seconds would be enough. If you came, I'd falter;
the crook of an arm, our hands tangled into one another's all wrong, like we've forgotten the use
of fingers. *Where have you been?* You don't wanna know. *Do you like dancing?*
I do a great lap-dance to *The National Anthem* from *Kid A*. I swear. I never lie—

The flat is fleshed back to wires and noise. The sun takes the plaster in its fists then the ghosts.
I woke up and thought the day might go on forever. I died enough times to know
my mirror image does me no justice. I'd like to see you in pain but I don't want you to suffer.
When you grabbed my legs and forced them so you could fuck me harder and I felt your hard on
God so huge and hard I thought I might die if I touched it, and we freeze there.
Anaïs Nin, you only wrote that stuff for money. Well I only write to feel—
and it elicits and evokes; cum, turbulence.
      Down to the foundations, I know the ground has blisters
and there is no such thing as morphic resonance around here. The city doesn't remember Dickens,
it doesn't remember murders; the body in the suitcase in Clapton found its way to the morgue
like everyone else. Someone pieced her back together best they could. Mark called me
on the ward; I told him my ex-husband is a fucking coward. I kept having to light my cigarette
in the rain, and yes, despite everything, I am loved.

My last lover told me he'd thought about what to do with my body if he killed me.
I laughed and told him *where the fuck will you buy lime*? We only fucked when he was too tired
to haul my corpse anywhere. *My flatmates will hear*. The walls are plasterboard. We come quietly;

but we will. And I have lost all sensation in my apogee. Meridian love;
if you don't wear gloves I'll feel safer. Keep your eyes on me and don't lose it—
God knows about the pain when you look away and the hit comes. And the hitman comes
late. You know what it would take to protect me—me being something more vacuous.
      Bury me in a wicker cage as the sun goes down.
I don't just want to be beautiful in your gaze I want to be implicitly present and spacious.
The chord change makes me look over my shoulder; you see me in the mirror,
I hold the scissors and cut your hair close to your skin. Ah, and oh, and do it again, for Holofernes.
Maybe when you're old you'll realise what this meant—in a world where war doesn't *happen*
it just rapes spirituality until no one cares if Mars is habitable anymore. War's coming
and my name fades out on the paper for the last time—look back over this dreamland manuscript
as the last peel of bells calls, as the last fever takes the last baby boy; the ink dries, and look;
      as the flesh understands its agony, and the humiliated forget how to cry,
my little room is Auschwitz, yes, but it's also another planet. Where you're from
we can negotiate the price but not the value. I'll tell you a story to put you to rest—my lungs
invest in poison because finitude is comforting to charismata like us.
      My darling, where should it end?
A twelve-hour flight and it comes again. Around, you'll come around. Lovers like you
never die—I'll immortalise us both like the poets we are. Petrified now, the body rises to its equatorial zenith—apologies—
now alive, we can't be missed, but miss the things we trust are there, more than we miss the things we lose.
          The shift in light captures all the prayers I ever uttered. I miss you;
but you're carried. Teenage love songs through fluctuating time zones reverberate
as melancholy offers its hand
and I step out into your Canaan.

Transmigration of Souls

East wing, gone two in the morning, again; eyes croaking with pre-death and I alighted each platform looking at your feet.
Doubt. Peacocks like swollen glands on cream linen with a tassel-hemmed sash confuse both windows in this lounge room where you sleep
by the wood burner I lit and tended for you so the cold wouldn't reach your dream sequence. Your brother is there and he cares less and less.

No drill to wake for; we barely rise 'til noon and still beyond is simpler. Astounded by what we want as though it's a novelty to want at all.
I think of the word *fantasia* and apply it to our mansion villa—no idea how we are here. Don't ask. Discard evidence, who needs to know and
you breathe too-contentedly and I feel guilt from stopping myself coming and stopping you. Pinching your neck by accident in the throes of having—

I don't know how to take. I don't know how to ask. I give. I respond. I think I look awful when the sweat sugar-soaks my too literate face.
Pancake flesh, a contained world of its own pang. Yes, I writhed like mad and the crickets were mating. I sucked all things inside and out.
I was a liver, then a kidney, then a mouth, then a throat and then I melted. Some part of me was a bed and something else a floor. No mind, but all worry.

I textualize sensation because it hurts to *feel* feeling. The anxiety of the Mother who is gone leans over the wash basin and sees the swollen chops.
All doleful my pupils respond madly to the light after the emergency methadone. Oh, when it's in me I have a bug. I bite everything and nothing tastes good.
But you taste like a tropical-marine ultra-sensitive seabay doublemastication salt-eel wallpounding. How did I get off. Your pupils moats of snot-green but dark-

hazel and moated with ecstasy. Where is the *more* I rowed in on? O bravery, bravery, your white lace babydoll smells like an upper-class whorehouse now.
Black velvet corset on the bed. Requesting the tying-in but all of the pieces float apart whilst we consider the aqueduct and both think of suicide simultaneously.
How far-away death seems when you are in love. Three times today we sensed the drop—Grenfell Tower; char of violence with *yawn* a gouge of gag.

Sightseeing and pencil-lead. Buried under your nose I make myself erupt. I'm not ample my darling I'm obscene. I cut a piece out of the dressing to reveal
a nipple still wanting for a suck. But it's ever so sad and I can't look at it. Massage coconut oil into my vagina as I do most days because it keeps me lithe.
You like the word lithe and I like the word bedrock. Do you think she thinks we're commoners? I know her and she has incredibly thick blood but no skin to
    hold onto it.

I should sleep. Should stop reinventing twilight and dawn as though I'm separate from the machine which can only swallow our pennies.
My vowels are impressed by yours but can't mimic. Imitation is like infatuation, devoid of authentic philosophies. Five housemaid bells above my head
so the rich can impress on one another how great it is to never be subservient. And yes, ma'am, but you're a randy old bitch and I'd recommend stitching it up

for good. Well it doesn't stop hurting. M lays awake with a face of Parisienne delight at being reborn without lifting anything. His fingers are sockets and his
hands are polar coastlines sweeping around for the lexical debris that might make true the night that won't stop insulting waking-hours-of-virtue *yawn*
yes I know *yawn* it's not so awesome to be delivered into The Exquisite Headlong Rush Of Prosody. *My cock is huge today, it's like a piece of rope.*

And yes, last night I said in a room full of people I don't know but must live with 'well I'd be on smack if I were a Jew.'
I said it was the most awful comment I'd ever made but that wasn't true whatsoever. Illness makes me more and more offensive; I stop to look around.
All those things I used to *think* and not *say* and now I split my lip trying to keep quiet. And currency makes up ninety-eight per cent of my body.

Coppering up for a ten pence Danish pastry. It is true that it's the poor who know best how to live. Somehow I don't remain dead when I die in my sleep each
morning and birds lose the plot as another plane shrugs its ugly carcass into Heathrow. Geographically, my love, we're close now. And
my love detonates in your pupils whilst a National Rail coach somewhere cleanses itself with more vomit. No more—you'll come with me

Barcelona, my nightingale. St. Petersburg on a whim. Tangiers. Penniless I brood over things I can't do and yet all things happen to me perhaps because I will
hard enough. Perhaps because I touch everything and I touch the things I shouldn't touch more and more until a simple room-temperature sensation makes
my tits freeze and my pussy throb like a nuclear twitch. Put me out whilst the fire chokes on this clean ash. Put the dirt back, I need the filth of

well I'd come hither darling but for God's sake I am half dead. Nothing sexy about illness except that
you feel the well of dormancy.

Bleak Future Text

After ruining the dining table and remaining silent for the forty-minute drive I was sad to learn Oklahoma no longer serve the slick bourgeois tea, London Fog. And when David uttered the words 'wank room' in relation to the high-profile pornography-advocating writer I thought at last, a man who doesn't try to turn complexity off on cue // It's not enough to be what you're capable of, I tell myself whilst walking home via the phallus-shaped cenotaph—it's not enough to do what you are good at, but you have to go beyond it in order to prevent your own self-parody—and even then, as I saw my sullen, sinusitis-swollen face in a car windscreen I knew I was that parody, and that empty space, and that a grandiose self-belief, any self-belief—will kill even the least deluded amongst us // David says, your new style looks so good. And David blows his nose unapologetically and hard and formulates a river of lines of inquiry he'd had no counterpoint for and no way of expressing what we make, at best, sound as though it was conceived in a vacuum after a lifetime of sucking up to the man. And David's just about as sane as they come—analysing the fixed and rigged results of science experiments running toward, not away from, the bias of the desire of the fanatic to be the leading researcher in their shady field // And what's the moon? It is a shiny bright oracle inducing tidal waves and what do we know of it? And what do we know of the huge, new planet, mapped in the skies by physicists who haven't seen it—it's a blot, an emptiness, and what can we do with the limits of our knowledge—we colour in the cosmic gaps // Poets please find the *piano*, the *legato*. Find the crescendo, find the hot-spot, the abracadabra and the crushing blow to the unconscious that comes on the aural tide of a certain, grating sound. The cries of babies. The pitch of a supermarket security alarm. Find the alarm and work backwards—the gentler tones come only after temporary deafness. I hardly ever listen to my peers' advice, and they openly belittle mine // We are devoid of spirituality in a hipster bar, a couple of queers, then spirituality is devoid of us when we sneeze in reaction to aligning our sensitive moral values. And your sleep paralysis, David, and your nosebleed over the last verse of your poem made you see some sort of sense at the time which was why never to use language to fill a space that is there for a reason. If only I could atone for never giving that method a chance, for pissing in Time's cistern with enigmatic poems. What would Jesus make of this? Hard to say, time has passed. Mary thinks of the desert and gulps // There's a leak in the swimming pool of Hell. They wanted only academics in this year to enrich the fiery furnace so unfortunately for His Highness there was no one who could stem the drip. His delegates argued for several hours over ways and means, and lay down on couches, and prayed to the Heavens, and eventually fell about in states of ambivalence until some poor soul said, *we're just so over-qualified for this!* // Justice prevails whilst I go about paying for my Starbucks with a voucher I found in an undelivered letter in response to a complaint made by someone else. I love having things I don't deserve and never looked for. The Frappuccino is so cold my heart misses an essential beat it'll never get back. All those starving third-world children I duped out of two pence. I hope someone goes out there to count them and supplies accurate numbers // The liberal communists go down to the shooting range to ironically conceptually shoot their comrades, then go home to dictate to their wives an email they had been meaning to send to their competitors which detailed the exact amount of money they had given to charity that year, and how their competitors need to up their game if they are to compete for moral virtue on an even field. We're plying so much into humanity, they say to themselves beneath the power-shower whilst the electronic device screen blinks its blue-hearted hatred // [I look at the people chasing down the street after banknotes this Bank Holiday and fail to supply adequate commentary on issues relating to the economy I could slip in somewhere but have no real knowledge on which to speculate] I'm so over Judas. I forget I have a body, forget I own a purse // [*I didn't ask you many questions, I realised later; I was so interested in my own contributions, and you reacted in exactly the way I dream about people reacting to my expressions of disgust at the ineptitude of human beings in their delirious and conscious pursuit of mimicry as a crude form of justification of everyday crimes.*] They are taking over. And they won't stop. The rosewater cake is spectacular. I don't know what you really think of me, David, when I use the word genitalia and fill my mouth with bright pink fondant icing as if on some kind of double-entendred cue // Is anywhere safe? Ethical responsibility comes at a price shaven off the ever expanding ego—we imagine, David, someone effortlessly assailing you in the Fig and Sparrow, slitting your white throat perhaps never ever before having seen you anywhere—coming face to face with your assailant is so hard to do these days, it can't be relied upon in times of conflict, and who wants to see real blood when you could just stay home with a single malt whiskey and the promise of a late-night handjob, pressing unbiodegradable buttons // This isn't about me, is it, or is it? The writer asks me my last name as if to enquire as to whether the conversation has any real kudos at all, I tell her, I'm Magdalene. Mary. I want to be someone else, someone less oracular than me // Why don't you tell more stories, I wonder of the confessional writers whose authenticity is evolved from praying for oneself. What good is a poem if you're drowning in a quagmire of war, or living in a town full of pound shops? // You're silly to want more when you're better than yourself in a public forum. We were always going to create a world of screens on which to represent ourselves in better lighting. Our good sides are mutating into algorithms; in a few more years we'll be able to fall in love with our doppelgängers then lobby hard for self-self-marriage // Dear friend, don't apologise. I'm glad we talked at such length about this. *The moralist is bleeding. The moralist bleeds and bleeds. We haven't got any change. We are glad when the junkie at the cash machine is sleeping. The weighted words have such value in the free market where even the weightless find value in neologisms. Copy replaces copy. The antagonist replaces the affectionate clerk. The totalitarianism goes unnoticed, and I blush when I realise I've walked four blocks with my skirt around my waist. There's no picture opportunity sometimes and where's the justice in that? Your love is a new kind of terse and I like it—it suits our vibe—you frown and I pay the bill, and then we go our separate ways seething with unmirrored anguish. The tipping system is intrinsically flawed. All systems are corrupt except when you pray to them. Tiredness has not made me a better person. I spend my whole life writing an elaborate defence of my own work for its very last reader as poetry dies. The third world shrinks in comparison to the infinite pain of the stock exchange the day the ledger described an incomprehensible figure with so many swollen zeros the whole world went bankrupt, just like that.*

Beelzebub Has No Truck With This International Court Judge Says Tearful Witness And Adds 'Thank God, Amen'

then the awakening came a little after nine when I considered the subtext and its deplorable ramifications—I'd cornered your anxiety about being admired—the plateaux has no particular ascension or descent on Good Friday, at least not that I can see. The old white-haired Christian, walking with his enormous wooden cross, shoulders hunched, a red cape draped, his flower-arranging disciples muddling behind, reached the church where Bartholomew's rusted flaying knife is supposedly hammered to the wall, cringing, uniquely martyred. To believe you are a crucial part in someone else's story takes little imagination, but an awful lot of blind faith. We drive past the newborn lambs and I say, *your father says we're having sacrificial lamb for dinner on Easter Sunday*. He bangs on the car window to wake me from my analogue slumber, connected to humanity via an aerial frequency. I listen to *Bleach* on the second day of Jesus' death, consider Oedipus and Cobain, all the insufferable sufferers, and the incessant selfishness of my masochistic confidantes. Past thirty it's all about developing a more faithful and reliable complex, about constantly echoing the sentiment of your hated parent's, 'I haven't got time for this.' My patience waxes lyrical then dies an early death and I feel put out by having butter on my hands and not being able to reach the tap because someone else is washing up. I blow out a lot of hot air to make my irritation more obvious. All those poems I thought I was writing, had written, that are being read without my derision, oh Lord. The disclaimer states you understand your opinion counts for nothing *before* you read. If that's ok then it's settled. Ah the lambs bleat. The interludes between kisses are so unsweet. Consider the intersectional nature of politics in between our eyeballs—we see in our limited field of vision the rolling hills, we see our rapidly aging skins, and we have to conceptualise our political persuasions amidst gorgeousness. How the world makes ugly what it cannot kill. How God thought fairness could be replaced with wrinkles I have no idea. If he really has white hair maybe he finds us more beautiful in our maturity. I can't complain yet—nothing sags. My dog has fur all the way up to his eyeballs and the LSD flashbacks make me gawp idiotically. I spend most days under the supervision of embarrassment. When A took so much acid he spent a whole week locked in a bathroom in Hell he dignified the telling of it with humour. Then when he cut the phone lines and destroyed my house he justified the telling of it with confession. And when he finally saw red and raped me he never spoke of me again. A Facebook message after several years denotes a definite shift in conscience, a phenomena always open to editorial changes. I'll never be paid an advance for this. I'm leaving to go and make art out of someone else's nothing. The students make more poems in the style of their teacher, and in another time I am flogging myself through the streets, burning incense, over some minor offence I committed in writing down unforgivable sentences. I wish I was a writer of hymns that take several years to learn the melody to sing. My mother-in-law's new wig is rain-proof and my skin suffers the terrible osmosis of self-consciousness and weeping and my eyes are still swollen from the afternoon I spent crying over what I don't know. Pre-Raphaelite babes look completely vacant and nonchalant in their nakedness or luxurious robes and I take an awful photograph if I don't smile. I hate the word facial. My face is one sulk away from stupor. Radovan Karadžić gets forty years pre-crucifixion after representing himself, cross-examining the witnesses whose parents, wives and children he murdered. On Newsnight I watch boys being gunned down in ditches. We're so removed from humanity that video images of first degree murder cease to affect us. I wonder who will be the first to hang when we get a grip of our concern about becoming notorious monsters. If God is listening then make those war factories supply more shackles. We demand more rights only when they are impinged upon—the war-tsunami on its way to break over the world will not restrain itself if we protest it. My nieces say cute things about cats and play charades and Sweet Chariot badly and I sit amongst the wreckage of my sister's life and my ineffectual dismay multiplies. They mime the turning of a tap, then the peeling of a banana. I say nothing, I don't want to play. I hate kids. I'd rather grate my own fingernails than entertain innocence. A fifty-pound stake on whoever can make our dog sing results in the weird, competing howls of our children. If only the newsreel would stop and I'd sleep and Hugo Ball was not so serious as a young man and we didn't see the funny side in an old sycophant climbing a hill in a broken working-class town carrying his own cross and if only my sister's citalopram had not provoked her first religious experience. If only I'd reached the age of thirty-three having had no near-death experiences or hallucinations in which God Himself expressed his encouragement of my forming a new wave grunge ensemble with the specific aim of uniting civilisation. No one that day understood why

I sat on a bench for hours singing a song I'd just made up and banging imaginary drums giddily on my chubby knees, smeared bright red lip gloss across my face and attended a session on John Stuart Mill in which, when asked to read aloud the text I put my head on the desk and wished I never had to sit up straight again.

And Anyway, In Light Of These Recent Events, I Don't Even Know Why I Came

What hunts you, little bird, the writer with a beakful of prizes? I could've let the train run through to Manchester and instead I'm coming home to you. I bought this for you overseas—to save customs seizing it, I tied it to the back of this pigeon with a little love note and a love-heart like the Smashing Pumpkins' nineties band logo. It's been a long time coming darling, be really, really careful with my long-form tired kindness. It's a meaningless transaction to give love-gifts when you could have spent your youth making bombs described in the anarchist's cookbook and joined a militant regime, such was the dream of many teenage stoners whose parents' primal sex romps haunted their formative memories. I place shiny coins in the palms of the destitute who have to wear placards describing themselves as 'British and Homeless' now we are living in the Age of Idiocy. The homeless feel the implosion in you through me. I channel the spirit of a broken necked acid trip pigeon as a teenage runaway sat on the pavement of Chorlton Street Bus Station. I took so much acid I couldn't remember having taken it and for a whole hour I absorbed the energy of a metamorphosing pigeon whose thousand pecks at the ground broke its neck. Its neck-bone protruded bloodily as it grew to the size of the now ten-year-old child I later had. I don't fear anything, and I don't feel anything either. Do you? I'm the size of a small family car, silly. Sitting naked in this pristine budget hotel at four in the morning eating a warm lemon yoghurt with a spork. Nobody does it like you, eh? I absorb the impact of a whole nation's violent and bloody diarrhoea. If the very rich and corrupt can look pretty then I haven't got a chance with my stretch marks and self-harm scars that tell others I was once a juvenile delinquent with an exaggerated self-awareness that first got me into this mess. Pigeons in city centres trip me out so much. You carried my dynamite bundle so far with your stoner flick lighter ready to ignite it. On Monday I said how about it and we walked up the lane to the reservoir at dusk and smoked our second spliff in ten years, though you have smoked alone for decades. It tasted like shit, it honestly did. You laughed about my ladylike way of holding it, in between my fingers, away from my face. I told our sheepdog not to tell anybody and he said he could keep a secret. You said you felt less paranoid than you usually did and I wondered why you ever got a kick out of it. I'm on this train at six am even though I could be in the hotel room I paid for and booked to sleep in, and don't have to vacate until eleven. I rang you at five am having printed a mini statement for the ATM experiencing profound psychical alarm at our bank balance. I said a hacker has drained our account you said no, you spent all of it. I paced around Platform Seven swigging a blueberry drink with the words FEEL GOOD emblazoned on it. Ah, come on, it's not the weed's fault, I've been mad since the eighties. If you want to blame anyone blame the government. I took three sleepers at four in the morning and forgot, and just hallucinated a man sat across from me on this train explaining he is going to remove his pants and eat them. Good lord. The delusional shouldn't be allowed to purchase tickets. Pigeons remind me of the theatre we live within—even our most under-performed moments are implosively over-performed. I was sick three times this week through pure incredulity. And if someone you don't like tells you to bend over you shouldn't let them fuck you twice. Something might perforate within. Words like 'cockshiner' are funny enough to exist without a context, whereas my name, out of context, is the plot device of a gender-bending, comic-subversive, meta-fiction narrative. A bad childhood is still a childhood. Invalidation still contains the word validation. You avoid loneliness like a militant psychopath. Don't leave me alone this way. I can hear my own pulse when you are not there. The pigeon hunts down a sausage roll fix on Platform Fifteen as I struggle to stay awake on my feet. The music video that exists adjacent to my life is so much better than the melancholy aesthetic of the endless anticipatory goodbye through a sublime early morning rainstorm. If I don't want to go somewhere I just shut down. The sweet skills of the dissociative never win awards. The camera pans in on the face of the loser whose lipstick has been applied and re-re-applied. I've been awake for over twenty-six hours and I'm only getting crazier. I sat in the hotel bar of the wrong hotel and a kid in a Bulgakov green shirt served me English Breakfast Tea in transparent glass mugs explaining that they are only allowed three stars because there's no phones in the rooms but they're such nice staff so they should have more stars. The imagined uniformity of consumer experience delights me. He looks longingly at my literary award in its glass frame and tries to remember my name. He describes his socially deprived background with an unsubtle hint of shame. What an absolute phoney I really am at three am. I tell him he probably earns more money than me but he shrugs embarrassedly. Poets consume way more than their illiterate peers is what the tabloids are saying. Loneliness escalates to worthlessness without a chemical antidote. I look so fucked up in this decade old dress I probably didn't even wash a decade ago when I last wore it to a wedding where one of the guests committed suicide shortly after leaving. I had a temperature and all the writers who clapped me on my back had to wipe their hands because I was sweating so profusely. I keep convention in check so you don't have to. Your breath in my face was actually not that unpleasant. Happiness lay down on the tracks several years ago but lay the wrong way and the train just hurtled over. I travel through the tunnel of a magic mountain and emerge in the wilds of Lancashire. I make spells to dis-exist. I'll send this poem by carrier pigeon through a war-torn country post-haste. There are no release doves in working class towns you middle class lunatic. The class war is an absolute riot when you come from the roughest South Manchester council estate and have to plane down your rough edges to compete in the literary market. I wouldn't even blend into a camouflaged battle scene the way I blend in at these prize-givings with too much scarred flesh showing. But I won't do selfies with desperately attractive novelists. It wasn't in the contract I signed. Border control have developed senses that detect unusual levels of enthusiasm in immigrants. I eat a huge hunk of deconstructed beef and realise it's nothing more than tinned processed meat on a fine china plate with some weird jus and sip my prosecco. Writing this sure beats giving handjobs for a living, though I realise I do nothing more on a daily basis than sell myself for less money than I'd get through prostituting my body. I'm not muscling in on your beautiful lesbian girlfriend for God's sake, can't you see I'm drinking cheap piss pints of cider with not even enough brain cells to make a coherent anti-sex work argument. She doesn't even like fatties. I'm a sad recreational prescription opiate fuckmachine and even the mortally lonely won't have me. I wanted to suck on her superior quality *paramour* vape. We all have a finely tuned recall for graphically desensitised sexual images. Imagine if you wanted a wank but had to wait several months for a suitable image to be delivered by carrier pigeon then get it through customs. In your final year of high school now they give out questionnaires with questions like, 'if you could round up a particular minority and put them on an island and bomb it to hell which minority would you choose?' I'm sure most people would have their favourite but I'm thinking no one has yet picked 'the enthusiastically fatalistic nihilists'. No one can annihilate those fuckers. The sun comes out as I arrive home in my alien state and cry because I have a fever and have been tripping for the last four hours. But this particular poetic shambles is nothing more than a flake of dirt in God's good eye. And the pigeons can't do a thing about the incessant downpour. And I can't do a thing about telling strangers aspects of my life I've only hitherto mythologised for the purposes of the artform. I dream about the Love Songs of Boris Johnson in which he does a cover of a Womack and Womack song. And yes, I really am this fat, and yes, these gingerbread lattes will kill you sooner than a smack habit, and yes, you'd also look this fat in a fat-suit. The soldier in the hotel lobby explained that female soldiers don't even have to go to war. They can actually stay home with a laptop and hit enter to drop remote drone airstrikes without even having to feel bad about dead children; you push a button and your children eat the best organic food. I choked openly on my overpriced, stale panini as she told me this. I thought about reiterating Adorno's most quoted line but could only weakly utter the words, "I don't know anything about war." I footed the bill though she had asked me here to pick my brains about 'female war poetry' whilst Nicola Sturgeon walked by the building with her press team in six-inch prick-compensating heels and a cobalt blue bodycon dress. Her pigeons have been bred to storm parliament next time we're in psychic corporate meltdown. An insane sugar addiction has given me a cosmic comedown for the foreseeable future, and a prolonged hangover period will undoubtedly make this new reality ever more ever more cruel.

White Nights

I'm not going to sleep without you.
I lie here with seven books crushing my chest to stop me rising
from the dead. How the nerves of others flay me now.

On the Atlas Mountains, the freshly buried dead
were weighted down by white rocks. Who wouldn't envy them?
Sunrise is no longer postcard-worthy. *This fucking burns me.*

The lie beneath my bed has not grown since the last scan.
The cancer is not trying hard enough.
My interview featured a trigger warning. If you're sensitive

the ground will not swallow you at will, and you may not want
to come back. It's a burden to be this irritating to others.
I pay the critic out with a smiley face and thirty-four years of inner irony.

I feel such joy when I waste your time.
Your time is not as precious as we imagine. My time
is less precious than yours—I don't care how you use it,

as long as it's used with vigour. Mark
keeled over and his purple tongue melted. We all take
too much.

My lungs are pockets of inverted poverty.
Think of all the shit that's rubbed up inside them.
It's perverse that we corrode so easily when we try so hard to live,

but when we try as hard to fade, survival's incessant Christ-complex
pulls us back on our feet and hands us a prescription, and for what?
And someone better placed and better paid can do it better
and with less enthusiasm.

I sit in the waiting room where a poster reads:
forty million pounds is wasted in unused prescriptions each year,
I think of all I stole, cajoled and misused in the name of imagined science.

Huffing glue in the absence of absolution.
The placcy bag heaves like the world's oldest man's lungs.
No matter what happens the chlorine burns

children in Syria because it can. We haven't the energy.
We check one another's vital signs every four minutes.
She looks at me amazed and tells me we're not dead.

No one has a solid reason to trust in God.
I use words for remedial purposes like a junkie uses fire.
It takes me all day just to defend myself.

The money sounds nice, but I'd like to still be able to walk
if at all possible. Basslines and misdiagnoses.
You can't refute the educated opinions of the educated.

There are no letters after my name, just the wizened regrets that lack
symbols. You get stuck in one position when the wind changes then
have no room to talk.

There are always two chances if you count love and death.
No matter how sudden it comes I always look around
to make sure you didn't see me crumple into this crux,

and fold, and I hold my phone in this thunderstorm,
rain running down my forearm, and I laugh when I tell you
I've had enough.

The Distant Mirror

Did you know I couldn't last?
I looked long for the mirror;
Mother,
        I have something important to tell you. No,
        There is no shame in it, perhaps. In the night,
        I chop the serpent and feed it to the children.
        Their sides split with black worms. Black oil runs
        From their eyes. I have these nightmares,
        Food as poison; bodies as disease. The heart's not
        Permanent. The ground beneath my feet is always
        Changing, sometimes not traversable. I can't
        Bring you to the dance. I did not welcome sickness—
        I admit there was much harm done,
        I grew a stomach for a brain.

        In destiny, we always find the short-cut.
        In Hell itself there is no music but
        We have to dance.

Winter dawn puts me back in the shelter of sleep. The volunteer driver takes me via the longest conceivable route in the rain, everything a dirty smush of brown. Through Rossendale, little Hamelin, where I hid with my sister, we climb Casterton Avenue, my fever steaming the windows. My mouth is very dry; I walk to the clinic looking for the jugs of cheap candy-sweet orange and blackcurrant—diluted to nothing. Sweet teeth gave me years of disease. My sister touched nothing. The shutters are down, there are builders fixing the fallen-in roof, electricians mending the circuits, but no doctors. I walk past the chemo lounge, where there is always someone leaving, clutching their belongings, hunched. It's closed. I go to the radiology unit and find I'm someone else. Wrappers fall out of my pockets, I'm seven again. A sad-looking blonde tells me to leave my clothes on the chair and I lean over the scanner. She takes this breast in cold hands and pushes my shoulder, pulls my arm, straightens me, goes behind the machine and takes a picture. She moves me and takes another, until I'm shivering and ionised. Does it hurt? No, no, of course it doesn't. Everything has already been touched; I pull in my atoms tight, the thought that I could be absorbed, slip into the blue-grey décor, disappear—I live as though my death is endlessly routine, half-clean, impersonable, freezing.

At home I show you a map of Australia the doctor drew on my breast in permanent marker.
At home I start to dance, we spend our hours seeking respite. I mend everything, a stitch at a time.
For days you ask me, how's Australia? For days the edges of the map dimple and fade.
The snaking scar running across the other side of my ribcage is nerve-less. It's just the way it is,

It goes unnoticed. They say symmetry is beautiful don't they? A symmetrical daughter
Is truly the antidote to failing, Mother said. I give meaning to my body. I mark my own limbs.
The drugs have me chewing my mouth, have me dreaming of my ex-husband,
Who calls me *sugar-tits*, who always wants proof. How do I explain unratifiable feelings?
You're either dying or not. We're always dying but you are never satisfied.

> *You will not see yourself, in the irises a shadow moving over the bed.*
> *Luckily there is this distant mirror. Here I watch it, fascinated.*

Remember in the back seat of the funeral car, me and you, Mother.
We sat beside Death together, for the first time. You were angry
That Death can never be private. A vultures' performance. Your father
Rattled in the oak box and wouldn't be buried. The sharp smell of carrion.
The road was worn, there was nothing to be done about our path.
The other time you didn't let me see our Father, his heart failed twice,
Once for us. He died alone, and silently. In Colwyn Bay, just he and Candy,
Overlooking the old sea. As though persuaded by a tide,
I turned to you, you crossed your stiff and suntanned legs
And recoiled at once. You said my lipstick was a shade too dark.
I think you must know; when you are dead, you have no mother.
My lovely, little fatalist.

My only Mother,
      We can but try to prepare.
      It goes on and on. The time you cut your finger
      And we were ushered out the room
      Because you started to cry.
      I cried because I'd never seen you crying before;
      My sister went white from shock.
      I made her suck an imperial mint,
      The sugar is the thing that brought her out.

> You helped them take the baby out,
> Fifteen hours I tried not to think. The clock
> Had stopped one hour in, the other hours were blank.
> It was a dance and I did not tire; I am still afraid.
> The baby didn't cry. The white women filed out.
> I begged the doctor and they gave me a mask.
> I lay there sixteen and tearless.
> *Cut it in two at once.*
> *We must do a Kandy dance,*
> *Smacking the heels and opening windows*
> *The soul will fly out.*

Dance—you have known how all these years. Mothers are born knowing the steps, but not how to end it. When Sandra tried to kill herself you barricaded me inside her house with her children and my baby and left us. My dearest, iridescent, pain-relived aunt. You said she was bruised all over her chest, so bruised her chest was purple and shining. In the night she had woken each of the children to say goodbye to them in turn. You leaned over her and told her my baby was the picture of health. I'm sad we made you wary of death. She drank, and you buried. Death placed the cuff on her wrist; and carried her to the steel drawer. And I, your terrible daughter, chose the asylum when I needed it. I just wanted the ceaselessness to be also *absent*. Everything there was blunt. As though you stole all the corners. You might have visited but your anguish wouldn't.

> *Kandy on the lawn, on the hockey pitch,*
> *Kandy dancing round the old man, making him mad—*
> *Kandy dancing off the cliff…*
> *Kandy making way for us to spin,*
> *As far as where we started.*

There is a story, and a reason why I had the fate I did.
You placed the mirror by the bed although I always turned it to the wall,
To hide the things I saw in it.

I had anaphylactic shock from a can of Coke; I was amazed you hadn't expected it. Whirling in a fury of sugary caffeine, falling down. Right away you panicked; you watched and no words came out. I had been a given, sweeties in my hair, roses pinned to my coat, an entity proved not to change—a child. You roused the family doctor to rush to my side with his flea-eared bag and he stood beside my rigid body whilst my late father explained, 'she's going to die', and thrust the needle into my arm. Foam dried on my mouth; a sense that something inevitable *had not happened*. I recall only a certainty of death, which seemed so cheap, so naïve, so frankly pathetic.

And all the while I have to love, and I have to love to make the dying difficult.
My last four things. Norman's chamber. Swinging from the cherry tree; ever so stoned.
It has to be an arduous thing, to live: to prove you had existed. Love is splendiferous only
After the event. I don't doubt I will be loved one day. Perhaps if I think of you too often,
You cease to breathe. Perhaps you will become a Saint. Dying on one plane,
You sleep well in another. You check the tank and drive for another few trillion miles.
You sleeping beside me. If only we fed on the same sunshine; the sun alone.
Somewhere, my baby dances in her white dress, made from my million motherly stitches.

> *There your reflection, over the sea, behind the moon,*
> *Out there so you do not see too much. If you could see that far,*
> *You would stop looking. You would curl up and sleep,*
> *A little nebula of future dust and old stars,*
> *Clinging to itself.*

When you are ill, you have no mother.
Now the bones are all but healed,
The doctors are doctoring,
The space between the bones and the flesh
Is full of holes, imperceptible holes,
In the cells, emptinesses,
Where there was sunlight—gaps.
Where the heart was envying photosynthesis,
Now it remembers its death,
Ten hundred thousand pangs ago.

> *Heel, toe, heel, tap. In silver shoes*
> *She taps until you remember how*
> *The soles of her feet sent ripples underground,*
> *And she slept always at the foot of the bed,*
> *Denying her cheek of a pillow.*
> *If I could give these dreams a house,*
> *I would make it without the echoes.*

What's in the papers today, is in the papers tomorrow. The sun fits.
Is it important to know you're right about the end of the world?
The tides distorting even our skulls; oh must you draw such attention to it.
The tides pulling at our brains. The pull of aeroplanes and skyscrapers.
You have these memories already stored, up in the places they found deficient.
They drain the cavity again; they perform an ethereal amniocentesis.
See how the lilies and the lily ponds curve. See how the frogs dissolve.
Inward, everything concave. I danced for you in the box room.
There was never only one chance. Whatever you remove I will remember.
When you are ill, you are a mother. You see the distortions. You must worry
Yourself, you must worry about your transience.

My friend tells me being ill is a state of Grace, but it must be a state of Grace
The body is as awkward to dispose of as stars from the universe.
In a powder blue seizure I see ourselves and every one of our moments.
Misty blues call from the eaves tonight; I slip beneath the water's surface
And peel away the bloody bandage. Grace must never be complacent.
And here we are, O latitudinarian, dear little grieving.

> *Here, the tooth of the Lord Buddha. There, the Virgin's*
> *Washcloth. In a little while you'll see the Sabre-toothed and mummified,*
> *But please understand, everyone died.*

Whilst Grandma's womb ate itself I was reeling from three bereavements,
 — Steve's black bed, Steve's black casket, some magic trick or other.
Steve, I was astonished. Invisibility was in your grasp! I am faceless now,
With spoiled teeth. The brain grows big enough to burst then malingers. In your garden,
I swipe all the daffodils, just like I did each Mothering Sunday.
If this light will not come in I intend to force it.
Oh won't you make yourself well?

> Doctor's busy, but lovely, you'll never meet her, she's great, she lives in a bauble,
> She lives off bouillabaisse, she overheats like a car engine, she never goes to sleep! Her purring engine,

Basketcase. Fruits grow from her fingertips. There is nothing unique about my case.
I was alive and then I passed. You know she hand-picks her patients.
Best ones are the ones that might die, then couldn't.
The ones that will die, they're second rate. A Pyrrhic victory awaits.
The clever ones—they have a terrible time living. I see you, peering over my thoughts.
They have kaleidoscopic ideas, then their bodies shrivel up to compensate.

To all of the sons,
My heart ticks past the hour
Doubled over I count
And have no visits.
Are you tired?
Yes I'm very tired. Very tired
And are you cold? Yes,
Very cold. Very very cold.
Churning with cold.
Cold belly, cold eyes,
Gelatinous, feint.
Yesterday I went outside
And the world had changed.
The sun was in my eyes,
My dead dad was busking,
And the three o' clock light
Simpered,
And I avoided junkies
For the first time.
I keep my gaze to my feet,
When I caught sight of myself
In the shop window,
I hadn't seen myself
In so long
I had a shock.

Tales we tell ourselves are to bear
All the pains our parents couldn't
Can you hear them echoing back
From the distant place
You cannot go beyond?

In my bones, I have always loved Death, and always envied it.
All the comas and the lock-up wards only to find much later
I wasn't as unkillable as once thought.
          Mother,
This is my only letter, and when I sleep it really seems that nothing hurts.

In a dream I had built a palace.

FERDINAND CHEVAL

*… let me warm you
in a palace of pale blue ice!*

NIKOLAY NEKRASOV
from *Red-Nosed Frost*

Ideal Palace

VOLUME II

Psychorrhax

Last night I visited the place that is not India.
There were no aeroplanes leaving ever again.

I've dreamt of you, each separately, so you go nowhere
Without me. I would like to give you things that you can take.

If you can keep. I lived in a town two miles deep,
Two miles wide. I walked two miles each day and cried

Thinking of every place that is not there at all.
I might as well wear carpet, perhaps an entire roll,

A magic carpet; I might go somewhere without you.
You turn up in the strangest of places, sweetness;

I don't doubt there are more islands we have not seen.
There are very many secret avenues here—

Ginnels, gills, whilst the place breathes in and out,
Big-strong, I listen to the soldiers shouting silly orders,

Stomping—and next door the mosque and morning prayer jars
With an oncoming war. We never leave our shoes at the door,

My house is filled with animals; some you know, some you don't.
Yes we were under the same roof once, in the same tropical collapse.

We were ferreted around. I wanted to seem like a ghost.
I wanted to, yet here we are. Bloated Moon's rolling around yellow,

And Carl's cat is mating violently. I think perhaps she died,
At the end of the street. The owl comes by and mourns.

There is so much violence I see it only now. I kept it, before.
I removed it with the daily spell, the daily sugary alms.

I have much on my mind. Are there things we should leave?
Is there a list I could make. Betsy with the Italian girl,

Pleased with her beau, plump and dark—an avatar, or
Something else. I had that coppery taste again. I lay on my back

Saying god god god. Swollen chest, pierced and holy
And struggling to pout. I always wanted a pair of lovebirds.

I always wanted a tarantula. Or leverage. I always wanted
India. I always wanted my father to come back and die

Properly. Have I ever been an absence? I mean truly, ever—
You can't go away so how can I. The dreams in which I love

Everyone are hardest and most vulgar. To love everybody
Equally and with equal fervour. I must be by now quite mad,

Forcing myself to look until the re-assemblage is so entrancing
I cannot see it again without intense nausea and blindness.

Should I return, and sleep there, and let everyone love me.
I like hiding. I have found more places to hide in my life than you.

Under the bed, inside the wardrobe, into the Naples moon,
The Sicilian moon, the gangrenous moon, the factories, the shadow-

Workers, the cemetery, the affaires. Be good to me
And face what you can. I can only perform to the best of my abilities.

I'm sure I'll let you down. It is not art, I think I was *living*,
I was entirely as plush as you are imagined. Glow-in-the-dark

Stars hanging from the ceiling, sticking to my eyes.
Blowing kisses to the pilot, and all the sleeping passengers.

A Comprehensive History of the Byzantine Church

I will understand if
Danger is very willing
Very very willing.

Very. Clifftop sublime
Plus my hanging onto boats.
Ravens and lifeboats

I have been sad and bad.
Spidery spools. Drilled in,
A hot and heavy wasteland.

Sea-lined.

*

Dear erotic splendour,
Your time is coming to an end. Icebox,
You got it wrong again, it all wrong,
It's bone-marrowed, marshmallowed—miserable
Lace-clad, hornéd fawn. I have the love of
Everyone. It's très transparent.

I've been touching you now for a
Very long time. I have knuckle burns
All over. I have grazed my charisma. This
Is a difficult time. No I can't look now.
Wanted objects and the chasm it takes
From me, when I should be *dans profonde* the chasm.

I am living the detectable shrug, delicious.

*

I have one love. He knows. He's jellylicious.
He is not dutiful to me. He's splendid. He
Knows it's him. I know it. He knows everything. Love spills lines all over.
Love is explosive. Love is my sleep spoiled like a week-old child-corpse.
Moribund love. You were gone. To be alone to be alone. It is not a great shame
Not a problem. It is pecking at a sofa left out in the sun,
Covered in lice and ravens. And then on a white film,
You talking to me from a place like sleep. Like sleep but
Headlining—*you are not asleep*. You are not awake. You are not
With me, in me or out of me. You are not lost babe.

You have meteorological love all over the place. You have
Contemplated love in its entirety, once. I have dabbled frequently in vice.
I have let monsters and whole villages into me. I am a veteran of *this*.
Many have not tried and failed. Many more with hollow blood,
Many times many times I have said this to you. God I miss you
God god god I miss you why is it? God answers in my sleep tonight,
He tells me when you're suffering. He makes it plain and hurts my face.
He disgraces me and sends me to the outskirts, metal-clad.
He makes me draw up my legs and hold the backs of my thighs.
He makes me scream. The neighbours are merely honest.

*

A whole body
Lives in the heart
It listens, foetal. Tight.

It shops around.
It turns cartwheels
At a particular sound.

It has limbs all around yours
It has aural tendencies
It has lips

It has. What does it have
It has nothing left it
Is trying to retort

To get out of it.

*

God is entirely circular my darling.
In his centre we make him happy.
Outside of God we do not breathe a word.
Not a word to anyone. But I tell him everything!
Oh but I do. He has room for more words I tell you
Words are all. Teachable moments. True love terrifies.
It eats you out. The shock of her, stood there, impassioned,
Scarred, already died. I have already died, and so the sun
Comes up blaring the only colour no man has ever seen.
My face colourless. My pink labia. My green-eyed mouth.
You could've been somewhere hitting it. You were in a cave,
It's a dungeon before you know it. Mount Golgotha,
M steps out from behind the boulder, toying with an idea.
Hm. He looks around at the vista. Only moments before he was
Not alive. He was in an artwork, in a gallery, hanging. He did not
Smile. He did not give a fig either way. He looked at what he knew,
He knew what I did. He touched my upper lip it swelled.
I woke up tormented, bruised, flayed and terribly elated.
I wanted someone to know. *I want you too*. I redact:
I don't need happy. Beach sky. Bedroom.
Salted. Curdled. Wasted. God

I loved you before time. You are
Forgiven.

Hindmilk

You don't want to know the things I've done
Do you? When my milk came in I was a doll, silicone
Tore up and yawning. I would like to take a drink of it,
Take you back in my body. I think I can see far—
Jade's milky guitar. Tapped out in the crucible of dopesmoke
With daddy's friends. Red tape and red pens. I became
Greaseproof. Months lying on the same sheets hiding
From you. I wasn't a body just the odour of one.
I stopped even listening for the door, it was better to be
Immediately alarmed than ready for it. If you knew
Where I come from you would make me tea in winter
And coax me out of bed with a million hail Marys.

There is no renege on my milkiness—and I lied. I saw you—
Both of us of striking bone in the other dimension fulfilled,
As though to fix something and stay immune, you hold back.
You must re-intuit. Together we would be alone irrevocable.
I said have your playpretties and snacks, all of it—
And your dubious liaisons, and your mouthwash,
And I'll build anything, whatever you like.
The sea coming up against the glass wall of salt and
Sharp yearning, never breaking it, fire of an ocean and
Something delicious living at the bottom of a
Crystal flute with your reflection tonight,
I am a kind of fruit, a mock-fix.

I saw a deep green around the edges of the tunnel
And a man in a green shirt pricking my little finger.
In a dream he leans in to suck the blood. In my room
He rubs it into a tiny machine. I slump listening to
Islands in the Stream, far far away. I hear you
Glugging in saline. Your upper lip the shape of
Some unfathomable sea-object, something priceless.

I can't afford it; the old man says watching pretty
Wobble away with his bottle. Time does not slump
Or move away—it moves in every direction,
Some you've never attempted. The felon in chains
Raves and rattles around the black peripheries.

Cigarette burns cascade around my line of sight
Where one door only closes, only shuts. I admitted.
The worst to him; I told him the thing I shouldn't write.
Anne in the Brixton room beside a wall of fern—
A pirouette and I need to fuck a woman. It's less
Annihilating for me. It's portentous and saturating.
But I want a man. I need a man. Unfixed and
Moving. Further than me so I can be the distant light.
To the very bottom I can see the spidery arms of sirens
And an ambulance flashing under the arc of the tides.
Down, in the short sight; I have been with you these nights
Hair in your eyes, the colour green, the smell of cinnamon.

My period smells like honey and heroin. There is still glass inside,
And green stiches all up my spine to my sternum
Dissolving when the cuffs come off and I go asleep;
And I go asleep. Panicked as a child that the blinkless moon
Would disappear and interrogate me—obfuscate me—
I have my eye on you, backwards orbit. I am always
Touching sand, I am at the baseline waiting, drawn.
By your attention I can never be lost or alone—
In the Elm Street squat biting my fingers. Devil in a
Cheap suit banging on the door I blocked the keyhole
With dust. When all the lights went out I could scurry out
Like a fox. Out there I only wanted to speak to you.

I'd dial random numbers to hear a voice. Here, there is
An object, a buoy, a focus, and I'm rained-in. My fingertips,
Did they graze it or did my mouth meet it too? A life of
Paraphernalia and back-street restaurants and insomniac
Loud narration over the spluttering world. Something is tight
Like a new bed. I am so over it. I am a cake, I am a
Litany, I am cherry-topped sundae, I am afraid of you,
Lopsided laughter like a baby with a xylophone—
Mopped all over with desire like disease. Crushing—
What do I regret, really. That lost entanglement perhaps—
The green quilt and the princess bed and me in a lift
Going high laughing at the green princess dress I wore to bed

When he said the words I wrote were silky I remembered
Why we no longer speak. *This* isn't small, so note that.
Skin so numb I faint just to think of it. I
Love. Take a book and press your fingers into all the pages—
Ask your sweetheart when it's going to happen. Undine whooped,
Virused and amazed it took so long—it took so long—
When I had the hook and my holy will was penetrating—
Still, it couldn't—time stopped, babygreeneyes I
Lost faith on the floodwater; how do I know exactly the size
Of you, your hand, mouth and the weight and the magnetic field
Grips—there is one line from here to there, just one.
You must stop absolutely everything and come.

Me & You in Ulysses

Stephen in the Martello tower crawling with lichen
Sack-clothed and we wait for the gurney. I meet you
For coffee and it hasn't rained all year—not like

We fix. It's rainy in Manchester you know.
Or wherever is *here*. You tell me we've been had but
I've known it all the time. Your shirt smells

Delicious. The blood isn't as real as it feels. You
Think we might hold hands for a while but it
Never comes. All night I have been lying

On my broken arm. Blood fills the skin indented
To the carpet. You are not tokenistic sorry, you are
Exhumed here. Over the sea from the sea-sprayed

Outer wall we can see there is no way home.
I say prayers for all the terrible ones making their
Solitary conditions inferior. I pin

Red orchids in my hair to greet you. I am
A good deal thinner. If you are saved, I understand,
I feel sharpened. I said some things today, regrettably—

But *I* love *you*. And that's the last meteor flying over.
The sea-spray makes us salty. You explain human
Nature to me. It's incredibly Napoleonic.

Drones fly over, made of plastic. We have all endured
A friend who has rocked us with turbulence.
Your head above the sea, your soft clothes

In my hand. I have premonitions, but that's
A tale for another Tuesday. Remember when soldiers
Used to come running toward one another yelling?

With silly tin helmets on? Cheering on the other
Team. It was at least colourful. Remember when we
Went to battle in our best zoot suits? You were not

Jealous of me then and you never have been. You were not
Even envious of my phrenic landscaping. You're dressed
Like Graham Greene and I am going to the cathedral.

You'll be shot and I'll die draped over a pew.
At least we won't be culpable, in dreams.
At least we won't be stoned to sleep in dreams.

At least the sea and sky will stay blue. Over Brighton,
Over Vanuatu. You see a rainbow that is only yours.
It doesn't reflect anywhere on the planet

Beside your retinas. Not even there, as it happens.
I want to see it so hard I'm nibbling my knuckles—
You tell me the blue is missing, the red and the

Yellow—you tell a lie to boost my ego and it
Doesn't shoot. Because the short man is coming over;
He's absolutely enamoured by this raw hot war.

He knows the last words of many men are 'mama'
And so we only nod and bray. When we win,
What is it we win? I suck on a drumstick lolly,

In a bombed-out pastoral scene. Death is only
Peripheral. I was all alone. And when you fall my darling
Out of the doorless door I am always here.

Galileo

White ointment.
I take your foot like it's a hand
Cure it, rub it, console it.
Your life curled inside the sole
Urchin—speechless;
You get growly on me
When I don't sing.

You're my Jim.
Everybody is my Jim,
And my husband is you and you
And my mother is my analyst
And my heart belongs to H.
You want to cure me and
Of course you do—

Your prayers don't help;
I'm saved. Monarch butterflies
Living in my shoes.
Ten-pound big boy boots.
Knickers digging into my buttocks,
I run far. You can't come.
I do not live for you.

*

We can carry the particulars across the cornstalk plains darling we can lug all kinds of things.
We can make fire and ice and drink rainwater and I can shoot things with my crossbow
At close range. There's stem-cells, there's morphine, all kinds of panaceas. You can cut bits out
You know. You can utilise radiation poisoning. And anyway it won't come to that because
I have too much to attend to. I can't find the time to whisk us away. To whisk you away
I imagine. Inconsolable. You all want everything from me you altogether do—

I can't offer an arm or a limb I need them. I need my own eyes too. I need braincells,
A roof. I need Timbuktu and a cantaloupe. I need pervasive, exquisite relief. I need you.
Oh my chest aches darling oh it does. They say appendages can press on other appendages until
Pressure builds up. They say it's too much to expect the worst and yet I should expect it.
They say I'm strong and brave and mad enough to take it. The rain soaks me see-through;
Quickening while the tractor growls through the mud. This twinge, my darling: it is not good.

*

What can I do?
Fixing to rupture,
Rouge & blanketed
Cells dropping off

        I can't remember what yellow is in French
        But this shit is yellow
        And you have to eat it all up for me
        Because I'm paid to make you eat it apparently

I had jaundice for like a day
I drenched the sheets last night
I said I wanted nothing at all
I ignored all signs and warnings

        You make me so enraged
        I can't stand up
        My pulse is out of time
        And the Earth is grinding to a halt

Because of you
Because you won't buy me a caravan
And you won't fuck me now
And you decided that months back

        Love is very pale
        The foxes are chasing the sheep into walls
        The badgers are out there digging their holes
        & I fucking love your fucking face

*

There were only two kinds: the predictable and the righteous.
Options were limited while the Venusian atmosphere blushed Day-Glo

And you stopped coming around. I hate to tell you this but
I am no lady. I have even contorted sound.

*

Please don't die horribly, he said.

*

At least your sex drive is still intact, he said.

*

Oh but you seemed so lovely.

*

The probe was in situ. We had an hour to
Phone it in. No one came running.
We spoke into our hands. Newton.
Newton. We pissed and shat ourselves.

*

I told you I regret knowing you because I love you.
You told me I was labyrinthine because it's true.

I will never, ever, ever come close to you.

*

I would stare into the sun as a child because I was told
The sun would burn my retinas and it didn't. Highly disappointed,
I cut myself instead.
                             And sometimes I'd climb and hang off
The edge of high-up places. Ledges. Roofs. Cliffs. My valedictory speech
Begins thus. *You are all cunts.*

*

They burn people like you: the interviewer refused eye contact.
Yes don't stick to your guns it only works as a slogan.
        It only works if you're twenty-two and big-titted and yawn.
        I could've been a fireman or made my money making porn.

Instead I made nothing making my life palatial. My life
Has been palatial and sighs right out of me in thirteen seconds.
        It ached and throbbed all night baby all night. In the morning
          A message came through. I said if you give them my name darling

None of those cunts will bother you.

*

Anne, I haven't written. You know that nothing has reached you.
I've been doing some time.
                           I would like to go now.
Right now I would like to give myself to you. For catastrophe's sake.

You've all held all of me; all different parts, all incomprehensible.
Kidderminster, Oxfordshire, London Boroughs—
                           Some of me in Lancashire, some scars.
I follow your prayers but do not rub along with them. I'm sorry.

To bring into existence this one thing: a train ride—and my Basquiat.
I have no money; limited time.
                                          I decided you a long time back.
I make decisions according to the vows inherent in making us talk.

*

If something is happening to you now
What a thing to happen to you now I
Think something is happening to us
While this is happening I am happening too—

And when I saw poor Tatiana in her flip-flops
Her skunk bag stinking up her jeans, I said
Oh my darling Tatiana darling come on in
And rest, Tatiana, anytime you can and must.

I carried her luggage up the spiral stairs
And when it killed me she looked so stoned
And vacant. I said I have something growing in me
Tatiana, I'm not even kidding. I can't breathe, you see,

Tatiana. And a man offered me experimental medicine
For free. And they wouldn't let me out of
The attic. And if I were worth more what would it be
To be of worth. To you. I can't cope I said I

Can't. Unchained I said I have nowhere to live.
I said mama I don't know why it costs so much, to
Live. And papa explained they had fucked with the wrong
Bitch. And I left Tatiana there appalled. All countries

Are foreign. I said goodbye and be good. And
Eat up all of your food. No one, no one sees me leave.

*

Bite down on that—I have irrigated nerves. Twelve-minute orgasms.
What do you want? I have about two pounds twenty-three and no time.
What can I do? Don't ask me. Darling, it's rude to not ask.

    I have no idea if this is working when it's working I ride back
    Shrugging, shrugging, with innocent Steve. I ask him if he's
    Ever seen a dead person he says I'm just a cab driver, man.

My Blue Beryl

If we don't have guns then is it really a crime? Just
Slap it and we'll be quits. But you understand the *import*
Of what's happening. Two wood pigeons cooing out of time,
The amphetamine psychotic gripping the steering wheel lets
The engine run while his partner dusts the living room in a pink
Chiffon gown. The yelp in the side, the ragged scarring.
A hope of hopes. The globally lukewarm condition—
Many more hours in the day than mathematically

Accounted for. Our lives are not-new and also, possible.
And I was thinking what to alter—one cell of two or
Whole corporeal structures. I was thinking all of a vividness
Of going blue. About mountains and mountains of you.
About joining the armed forces. Hitching a ride—I swear,
I swear, I have been this rigid before. I came out lopsided.
My lovely Basquiat, finding artwork in the loft. I was
Wanting so bad to bite that apple I woke up gnawing.

I might have killed for it. Instead I croaked.
And am I in your way? Oh I'm sorry am I in your way.
On the hook—read and bedded, buried and received—
Practically stoned on sentience. So *searing*, so encouraged—
A singular beansprout on a greasy plate. What a lot of ardour
For a presentiment. Fatherless, sadness. Child-friendly and
Finessed. Always walking home downhill and down. Christ I
Don't want to meet the parents. I'm happy. It's playtime.

Dimensions of butterfly wings, soft and luxurious.
I could put my mouth up to the glass and taste the coolness
Like this, and almost touch, like that, and rain will be falling
Always. Some perfectly aggressive sex and a busy day—
I need a map of it. A cartographer of internal organs told me

Things I already knew about frailty. Sometimes a pain
Buries deep and assumes itself a soul eating at your ribcage.
Should I write it down or shall you?

Manasa

My liver is a big ruby lake singing
With eels and brine. Sometimes
A shudder passes it over its skin
Like a wave. I think your head,
My boy, is calcified. You keep
Staring at your winning teeth.
The overlapping fangs, they turn
Inwards, against you. I knew
A boy whose viper tooth reached
Right into his skull—his eye-socket.
I thought he would kill me but was
Disappointed. The fire-axe slept
In its glass box. All around the castle
And the bay lit with fires and
The piggy-park, we philosophised.
We drank and gulped and plotted.
You smelled like juniper berries,
Anti-freeze and mushrooms.
We took ourselves to a little blank shack.
Slept on the flagged floor 'til our
Baby-bones shattered. My hips
Might have dislocated after the birth
Because of those nights. And there
Was something there—unbidden.
There was something. Behind some
Multi-dimensional veil, imprisoned
In the gutting room, not sleeping
Or moving, or whispering but
With us. A curtain of thinnest vellum—
An imprint or thumbprint or some
Shadow not ours. You saw the skeleton
Jolt on the stone floor. You had
Sucked up all the anthracite.

You had come very far. Redhead,
Shrinking before me. I packed
My cuts and blisters in clay, shoved
My feet into their combat boots,
Walked as far as I might—a weight
Like the yellow snake round my neck.
I drew in my heat, and took
Everything I wanted.

Clean Blue Night

I sorely tried to come on time but there was no wheel. It was
Watertight in there. I made up every name I could think while driving
And implored all the world leaders, their wives and in turn
I implored the bank robbers and snake milkers to come along
And I walked away leaving the vehicle trundling happily to its death.

Would you really and I mean *exclusively* want to walk about freely
In a world where everything you touch has a name. In a vision
I had three children with cinnamon hair and gave them all
My only living son's Christian name. The midwife said *but they
Each need different names to distinguish one from the other*, and I peered

Out the forty-fourth storey window into the cots and said
Dear lord you can *see quite clearly* they're not the same. I was mad
And thrilled and asked everyone I saw who named them. 15% of men
Were called John. Rattled and sick with longing I wrote to Matthew
Then Mark and Luke and explained I'd left the motor running,

That I could see no other excuse but to blame it on myself
And the immense demolition reminded me how easily I gloss over things.
Into a blue light where nothing has a sound. Nothing has anything like
A purpose. It was delightful and as real as Jesus and I can't anyway care
Even hear what you're saying so don't speak. You could

Just as well think it and I'd reach the conclusion. Remember, the planets
Fell into a big deep well and turned around until they fixated. You
Can't embellish something God did. If there had been a little more room
I might have loved more fully. I might have turned around slowly and
Looked over my shoulder lovesome. I might have seemed very new.

I might have looked very blue, with my mouth a little open with my
Dark blue tongue watching the crackpipe stars. Like Richard when he
Burned himself and I didn't think to tell him don't Richard it's useless

Because it wouldn't have been true. All these nights, motile—
Listening to the beery gable-owl and Chopin, worrying

Schopenhauer with my new map of me and the stars. Not only
A woman in love or even only a woman. Get me, stood here,
Staring at you with that look of wildly fragmented incoherence
Wearing it like a lovelorn Mary Magdalene all shoulders but without
The fragile beseeching eyes making it real. For you, I totalled it.

The car, my body, whatever. You can go see for yourself. It fell
Disappointingly into the sea with only a sizzle. I gave the husk
To charity and pawned the rust. I called my husband and the undertakers
At the same time. I made all the arrangements with a single thrust of
A red ballpoint pen. I went to my father in a weak gesture of goodness

And I coughed a little blood into his terribly dead hand.
Then nights with no circadian rhythm, quiet like a spell
In the mildewed cellar of your new home, testing the wires.
I can never unsee of your unimpressed faces. They have existed
Since God. I have taken us around the whole fluent sweep of Time;

I know sweetheart don't you worry I know. I hope the little fluttering
Accounts for my vigour. I know in a month or maybe long ago I will be
A single cell wrapped happily in a cellophane heaven and I will
Never provide. I unlearnt it all and went back to the beginning
Where the numbers are quite bestial. There was a zero-point field

With great style and it had all its arms in this one scene. How we laughed!
It put all its legs in too. It said there's no way out is there. Down
In the sunless well, where we harvest our wishes, the metal makes them
Weightier. Irretrievably Undine, in my tree-shaded escapade,
Neon, with a pimped red heart and spleen. We have to go search

Through all that is left. Hop hop; the road tar has scuffed the mirage.
If you're still at the station this late don't call just go on your way
To the grieving sea and think of all the things that aren't news
Now the cool night moves over. Roll your shirtsleeves and remember me
How I would wait for you effortlessly, any reach of time.

How I can still make a year last a moment and vice versa.
How I could take any room any place and be perfectly civilised
And not drown anyone, myself, or even flood the bathroom, often.
How I was young and magnanimous and appeared with a big
Red rosette as if I were the prize and your luck was all gone.

Original Mover

Something behind you
Clasps the light you leave as you move
And clasps and strokes at it.
In a little while there is presence
A priory presence—and I was there.

Light from a star
Milky with solitude and long in years
Came into my spine—I
Could see the way we turn
Toward one another when the sun lashes.

The churning of it makes a footnote:
Don't leave me alone—four faces
Exactly your own looking East and West
And North and South and un-cornered. Now,
Aroused by an original

Clay built, shouldered, double-mesmerised—
And without that light?
I was at your back crimping the shadow
Giving it ripples from the heart of the star
You are not descending.

Janus

I have conjured many things, Janus—lasting only brief moments;
Much has been wiped, and if I make myself recall—I can hover
Above, tracing the outlines. I have declined to live before—

And will not call, or speak. The two faces look in opposite directions;
Always—their landscapes cannot meet. I think of my childhood
In shades of yellow. If I travel there I go there bleached.

The mask of the woman has so many edges; octagonal, multifaceted,
Colourful and cursed. I think I do not smile as much; some force
Bends me to a ghost. I sit beneath the oaks, shimmering—

Water dripping from my fingers. I haven't been seen this month.
No blurring of the lip-line. Something harsher in my meanness.
For you, I hunt. I loosen the clothes and pale in the imprint.

A photograph folded down the middle—I have been folded—
I visit houses I've never entered, to see if the mirrors see—
Gilding the room with fingerprints. Crumbly hairs on the sheets;

To take apart all things in their separateness is a kind of art.
To have this face then this—golden forgery. I'm sick of reinvention,
And the liminal place where the shapes comingle,

Where things that are dead have lived before. Almost none of them
Shining. I have often paused, to make something stick; to picture
And frame the shot; you and your mouth and my head—

My eyelids give up. A dissolving image shakes itself right—
Unbearable now, to know what may have happened. In the gloop
And stickiness of sober images, I cannot mend the shadows

That stand where I might have been. If you could send me please
An aeroplane, some hallucinogenic drug—much extinction is manifest
In this comorbid world. When one cries, the universe does not throb.

I buried my first poem in a plastic box in the ground. I painted
Mad people who have fewer concerns. I practically wrote
My life for you. As though you might enter it.

Parallax

'Buildings undertaken and completed by a single architect are usually more beautiful and
better ordered than those who have several draftsmen.' — RENÉ DESCARTES

          She gave good utility—nimbly in the faux-wool sale-rail trench-coat
          Of another thin year she overlays all the whipped-up images of you
          One on top the other, until—something like a semblance
          Of pleasurable fury is achieved. 'She gave'—in the past tense.

          On the side of the sun where the skin dries, dust cells of bodies
          Settle in the condensation and I feign fun. Love is always prismatic—
          She discovers, watching it fly out at dejected angles. It flies
          Everywhere, she decides, and when emptied you have

          Nothing to chase. When I get some—I lock it in the blue box—
          More of a dart-frog blue than a honeycreeper-blue. The packets inside
          Are *almost-poppy*. We're back in the snow for lack of utility—waking
          In the dark she can't see can't make anything come. Pink palisades

          And palaces green-tinged by vacillating gazes. Thirty-eight years
          You turn gold around the pupils and no one explains.

Obit in Suck Magazine 1969

      I love you my little lunch.
            A pigeon carved into a loveheart by zombies
Waits with me by the road to the edge.

Do we live in Mercia? Come here in a
            Big black Pontiac and take me up Oxford Road
Where I used to do bad things during feral hours.

I sit across the sticky table tell you I'm nasty.
            Making plans all over the midnight blush
You say you keep having these head rushes; I feel it.

Vein-blue sky calling monsters outdoors; swallowing
            Cherry stones by accident. One moment in a fit
I deeply regret my feelings, thoughts and tendencies.

We're too much abandoned. It might leak.
            I hang the hoes in the office to dry out and scan
Inches, none of them real real in three dimensions.

We could go see a film—we don't have to talk
            Or look at ourselves looking for us. No I don't drink
I don't think. Too angry with dad. It bottlenecks in pubs.

In another sitch at the supermarket.
            Bleeding down my thighs. Magpies with crackpipes
Making houses of flytips. Bunny rabbits shaking their bustles.

What do you love about it? Do tell. My argument—
            Is against myself. Hoarding it all for myself. Tell it—
My sexual organs are all against it. They say I feel too much.

*

I can't tell you that.
A parody of a secret is a perfect nought.

I can tell you exactly what is was you thought.
You were terrified.

*

Distil your cum and saliva and sweat and blood and personal effects
And take me to the boat. No no no of course I won't
Rest my neck in the crook of your arm and breathe erratically.
No you'll be behind me but it'll be perfectly safe at night.
Who would do that? I won't crackle with tortured nerves of urges—
The sea will save me from yourself. It was oh it was cold in the wash—
No I went nowhere near you I didn't remove your garments.
No I was reaching I slipped. I just I got all full up.

*

You can kill one thing but not the other. One thing is okay to kill.
One is bound by secret legislature.
           Honey admit we have found the place
And are circling round and the nightmares are out of their dresses.

I can tell you don't need it. I think you know I do.
How oh how will I bear it?
           Toy animals frighten me. Inanimate,
Carnal. Trust basic bitches to take it back to the oestrogen level.

*

I would like you frosted.

Yes I would like you frosted and iced
+ I would like to lick the little sugar crystals twice
+ I would very much enjoy ten desserts.
There must be some ground rules or else
We would all be gluttons.

I kept it wrapped in plastic
In a black leather purse.
Every spoonful with a head-pounding thirst.
Now I need the sugar for a medicinal purpose,
+ I would very much desire to share it with you.
Open open open your mouth your tongue says so.

*

A satisfaction that lasts beyond the hour spreading itself before us
Is impossible. Oh so highly probable. My favourite is the gargantuan Sappho.
You're too far behind you need to draw it in with lustre.

He said he couldn't touch me if he wanted to, couldn't
Get his hand to connect—he said I pushed him away and his hand flung
Hit the table. He said how do you do that? That's it—it's there—

He pointed at my pussy and told me to use it. I stole
Many of his possessions over various excursions.
Still he didn't complain.

*

Chewing my way through the trenches, little by little I fed
        Rising out of the ground like a trunk, I climbed with my nails

To the top of the night. You looked down at my bleached face
There were feelings coming off of it. My feet snagged.

*

You cannot go.
I have no ears and no eyes.
Where will I go?

My hair tied in a knot of itself.
Spit it out now.
Skin is worthless unsexed.

A discipline must be earnest.
To be completely yours
Then at what cost.

We aren't *trying*
To fuck.

*

Never Never Never

    See it wasn't every day and you found that body in the landfill
    The seagulls were all screeching and the workers were bone cold.
    He was an interesting man. He had only one shoe on. He was always
    Too impressive; I fucked up.
                                  I fucked up first by being reasonable,
    Or reasoned-with; I was hurting—hurt. I was not sober if you count the
    Pain relief. I told a woman with blonde hair I could make her cum
    Right fucking now. And I didn't want to. No, I

    Wanted you. Tables, brains. A heart rate like a faulty metronome
    On poppers. No I wanted to fight someone instead. No I wanted to—
    You know I called them losers but what I meant was that I was repulsed.
    I was repulsed by that green tank top man—
                                  As a sexual object. Am I?
    You make me question how serious I'm being but I find always that
    I am. If you're serious get on the mother. Fucking. train.

    *

    Tummy cramps and a bag full of sand.
    Here, my love, hold my manly hand.

    *

    So this it spills into this and this and then I contuse into a barfight again
    With silicone Dave and his melted silicone appearance.
        Darling no you do not know, you do not know it. Let me
        Fill you right in. I had these dreams about what we are—
        We are not entirely turbulent.

    Sleeping through the deaths of parents of Gods of myself.
    The Narcan is cruel if cruelty is making life out of calamity—
        Is confusing. That's how we build a life; I have it planned:

You rest your head on my chest and stop breathing first.
First you stop breathing, then I choke it.

Yes but they're facts. They're facts and they make pictures.
Films are not facts built of pictures but we are though—if your
    Trousers smell dirty I'm all in for that; I'm all in for trust—
    A pair of wood pigeons make love-noises across a wide acre.
    They say 'You! You! You!' 'Never! Never! Never!'

And that's all we've got down to when the glass drains. Lime-rimmed
And our Latoya with her seven-inch curled earrings. Coca coca coca.
    Your million-dollar question doesn't come. I nurse the wound—
    I am your mum. I am your blood-coloured room. You are my
    Big-dicked horse. I want to ride you all over town.

*

Isn't it just for us?
Crack and rum.

Straight as a bent ring.
You deific fucking thing.

Run your mouth just let it run.
I rape you like a piledriver.

I lean in and garotte the bartender
To keep you close.

*

I watch *World War II in Colour*
To fall asleep.

*

It was all in black and white that place I want ten days I want a cache of interesting weapons.
I release you in the dark the baggage handler says the weight is just under. Not too light.

Have I gone too far again or is it almost morning and the southernmost tip of us collapses itself.
Not like a star, no, like an omen. I touch it and want and want and touch and bite.

There you go staggering into the night with your ripped open shirt and your fucked-up catechisms
Swirling on the girl. I have a tongue and you have a tongue. If it isn't wrong it isn't wrong.

How do things come so fast while you're under the table looking for the pattern of events.
My wife will be buxom and desireless. I'll finish her off when she starts crying about motion.

Should I bring beer or should I bring lotion. I will reinvent myself as a French masseuse
And never fall for the trick in the attic again. I will come down on you like a hooker full of Satan

And you say there's no comparison to be drawn. And there are hangers on and lookers-on.
And you say don't take any of these assholes home. Not now, not when you're drinking me.

Recapitulation

The smell of blood being washed away in cold water in a room full of metal.
If there's beauty, rewrite the scene: a beautiful woman washed blood from her skin
With cold water, in a room full of metal things. Did you imagine me then? My skin.

As delicate as ever I tiptoed to you. Tiptoed, from the shower to the bed. I tiptoed
To the bathroom. Around my feet in the cubicle the water ran red. Not wholly red, it was
Clay or mud. In reality, you are nowhere near to behold, so I forget you.

If I had not simply walked away from the accident, that time I strode across the street
Into the first bar I saw, where several men offered me drinks—if I'd been the victim,
Or the perpetrator, not the witness; my body was severed as a peach stone from its flesh.

Oh the cushy cushy world. Delicate peach of a kin. Have you ever buried a peach stone
Where it never stops raining? The mud clogs. I tiptoed out in it one night, to find my sister
Tripping in the garden in a storm, just as impossible to interpret as the formation of the Moon—

She described to me sailing; sitting in the soil, my toe-nails clogged with mud, menstrual
Blood down my legs. She said the world was all afloat. She gave me her oversized sweaters,
With the turtle-necks, to hide the bruises; how to breathe so *creepingly* to be almost silent,

Her little baby creep. We developed our pathologies non-synchronously.
My peach-skin sister, with her *Ambre Soleil*, her cocaine. A killer of small creatures,
A mother. She taught me how to mop the blood. She taught me about johnnies and lipstick.

How to close the wardrobe door from the inside. Why monsters prefer the cold and the dark.
Taught me to read, and look where it got me. The room was unsanitary, I thought of her,
I remembered the cars neatly parked by our mother's. Tiptoeing into a room where naked children

Cry for their mothers, for their meals. To be hungry, is it only a sin of the state. With the drip
In my arm, I knew I was out. I jumped the Metrolink and stood in the shower. I had just seen
Someone die. The baby turned over and the windowpane shook. More staples, more nails,

More drugs. The water is not so clean. The syrupy blood. I tiptoed, so they wouldn't guess;
Set my jaw to closed on its hinges, stayed perfectly schtum. My sister arrived stoned out of her mind
In a convertible sports car, that's all I remember. *If that was all*—Rebecca, won't you come back?

Professional Vs Amateur Wrestling

You'll go first

*

Every running-to has its hooves here, I spend an hour imagining the texture of the skin of your hands
Canal morgue shopping morgue bridge of sighs a courthouse four junkies picking out hairlice

Naked and nefarious. She wobbles over to the bench, turns and undresses across the street from us
Prison escorts prison vans a man in handcuffs the junkies wave their arms and ask him how long

How long how long. Oh poor Tom lying in the carpark lying in the dark lying on the tarmac in the sun
I don't fear death my darling. When you appraise me I fear living. Days fail me so I can learn — she says

It's all a con. She said the same when I lived in Aber aged twenty-one. Mama, I cannot surpass the bar
I have set. I looked and found you nowhere. Found experience like a found poem like a found

Mirage of the infinite futures.

*

        Siegfried, I never shut doors. I never
        Touch more than my share. I never cry
        I have cried oh I have. And you are
        Tilted on your axis so to look me up, down —
        A dart shoots around the world it misses
        My eye. It misses my thigh by a good
        Few hundred miles. Sunscreened lips
        And long strokes, and bite down on my
        Trapezius. For me bite down. I can
        Kneel and touch the ground with my
        Nose. All fours. Moaning desires. Honey-
        Thinkers. God-drinkers. I ferry myself
        Around on your heels. I am all ears.

*

Awestruck in an accumulated bunching of concerns about a shared skin—they wheel me in,
Pinched. We are confused in a plastic-wrapped way; afraid perhaps of our alternatives, afraid
Of acute bloodloss. The blood that runs downwards not up it is onto us.

Drill drill drill—what should I cut out to be of more appeal. Wainscotting and fornication—
Worktops and saddle-sores. I go about my business and my chores with a boned expression—
We should drink sangria all weekend make a tepee on a neighbouring lawn.

Strawberries washed over with cinnamon, and a half a pound of orgasmic plush. Tired I want
Your voice creamy, liable. I wish to be pliable. Hypnagogic and hearing voices. Dreamy man
In dreamland. If the circus comes to town I want to be riding that trapeze.

*

All furless, no tigers.
        The town turns on an edge
        I go to the well and make unity with fondness
        I light my 5p candle and keep on pacing
        Broadly speaking getting away from God my-
        Self a handful of moony inner thigh, a milky
        Borage. Starflowered arms, rocking my heat.

        Yes we are insane I know it—
        I have just shitloads of hypotheses—
        Can you meet me at Oxford station. Friday
        Brings no telegrams. What you do not wish to say
        You most need to—homes for beat-up children—
        This is not my home or my face. I am
        A permanent disgrace. Come burgeoningly to me.

*

What about my inner wrist? Teeth marks and smudges.
And what of the downtrodden in their purpled sleeping bags
Outside the burnt church, reciting cantos.
In the morning I found a used syringe. In the day,
A woman crawling in a carpark. In the dusk I found Catholicism
Waiting for a sock-it-to-em. Kind and fabulous prayer
Sending me asleep while the choir with their backs turned
Start bickering, and the church warden shoves
A golden fleet of angels reading all our all our books—
Toward the metal box to chuck our fifty pences.

Delicate imprints of oiled labia. Love turned inward—
Oh won't you grapple. My bemused scapulae
Watching the woman scalp me. You have me pinned,
Pined—pining. A triumph for the graverobbers—
Me all opened up and poured—a drink for mister
And a ghosted phonecall. Your head pounds. I thirst.
I have to believe you. The peroxide summer night
Bent over—breasts held aloft over your open mouth.
Coming for you now a vibrant pause while you
Collect yourself. Nothing more than corporal mist.

*

Indigo,
   Watching colour die
   And taste too
   Then aural craving
   Then bone-death
   Then death.
   Before me you have
   Gone wild on yourself
   I have been alone

I still am—freak
First flush.

We go beyond
Aubergine walls
Cradled doors
Melon flesh
Blush-streaked
Linen-wrapped
Like Jesus—bent beneath
The drowsy feet
All so hot I'm
Numen-awed.

Reasonable Doubt

An involuntary desire to live. These things exist
In the Bible. People trying not to die in old times.

Women trying not to live. Mist blanches the canal
That circles around our houses. Perhaps I am now

Childless. I didn't kill him he died. Life—
Killed him. Husbands with their dicks in everything.

Norma the ginger horse paddles about in the mud.
Frank the ginger cat loves the smell of fresh blood.

When I bore foetuses I couldn't hold on. I would
Grab my belly and pray to God. Grab my belly-fat

In clods. Raise my skirt and scream at the blood.
You are a very terrible husband my love.

Having become inured to barbarism, my arm
Won't stop shaking. The tremor is involuntary—

My arm wants to grieve. My babies want to live.
My body wants to expel itself. My hair is mad serious.

Love is not a pastime; it is not rote. Breathing beneath
An upturned boat. My Olympic heart rides out

My flipper feet feel nowt. When you first believe—
You are not loved one bit. I want to live in a pond

At the soggy end. I no longer wish to be convenient.
I dance in the rain in the night to evoke floods.

A water tower full of Barbie dolls. My sister shaved
Their heads to shame me so I sheared my own.

A boy tried to shame me so I made him cum; he
Shocked bright red. I don't care who wins anything.

If this were enough my bed wouldn't lean. I'm sorry
You do not know me at all—an unfortunate barrier—

Am I an accessory or on loan? I'm better than anyone
You know. My body glows in the dark bright pink—

Eschews fornications and gives great results—
I play the harp with my nipples. You were here

And now you're not. I can't even afford that bedsit—
Disowned: monsoons exist to have fun; satellites

Don't care who they orbit. When I started digging,
I was only twenty-one. I crawled across tables

In lace-trimmed socks. I was hope's hallucinated maiden—
A cracked rib enters the lung. I don't feel so well.

You hear that? I don't feel too good. I'll distract you
By modulating my breathing. My heart hammers

Like the almost-hanged. I've been cutting your hair
For years. You never stroked mine like a cat—

I will stroke you all over like a lynx. A pleasure must be
Merciless. I don't know where your body is, dad.

The town flushes green then begins to rise; bodies
Knock me about. My cracked humerus has not healed—

I jabbed a needle into it. If you could just make me vanish,
Would you do it? May I lick your lips? Bedsheets full of

Moth dust. I call and call the coroner to book a new
Appointment. We all shall die of unrequited hate.

Can I get a witness? I live beyond all reasonable doubt—
Barefoot out in the street. My monstrous grief is inviolate.

Palos Verdes Blue

Into the deer shelter he took me handed me to the sunrise through the square roof;
Ochre to begin, then every perceivable colour. I thought about resting—
It has been such a time since we sat together. His shoulders still hard I
Felt the cold. Turning up his collar he looked for deer trembling in the archways.

I used to see them, ears pricked by the land beside my auntie's farmhouse,
She'd raise the gun and *put!* I had no recourse there, she had all her barn-owls
Stuffed, she held a keen affection for death. I was to know, always grasp
They were rich and I was a bastard. Palos Verdes Blues pinned on white satin cushions

Framed above her bed. All the life we might have led without the sweetness. I want
To remember, Steven, I want to know what we did. In the shadows you might hear
The sound of their breath, the delicate hoofs. In our room does the light still subdue sleep
Through the gap in the curtains? Did Betty close her eyes and see you as she lost her sight?

I don't want to look at the moppet's new blue eyes, her new style of irate her cluelessness.
The new fawn in the barely perceptible light. Does she find my bed too soft
Or just right? Do you fear her? In the arboretum that November—I want to remember—
I can't. Milky prize marble baby eyes, your litany of regrets. There can't be a minus amount

Of love. I can be terrible here, distance helps the memory out of its sensorium,
There should be a word for how colour drains from thoughts of an ended marriage.
I try to remember; the deer stay hid, they are not careless, not even partly stupid
When it comes to us. Did you hold your hand out, expecting them to come,

To want to touch, so sadly hopeful? Imagine the musk and fur, the infantile longing,
The lust for all that is denied. A flash of white skin and your tan, I remember
Telling you I knew, she was blonde and inexperienced, so inexperienced I was
Eternally embarrassed. I was full of veins. She was salient, gauche, *under your nose—*

And Anne died at once so stylishly and with such panache. No I wasn't with her,
I could not allow it. I could not be reduced nor eclipsed by death or any disappearing act

But my own. You could have picked me up anywhere from Sparty Lea to London
Yet you left me to the hunted rabbits, the snow and the parties, the long years, dog years

Being shunned, the pawning of my wedding ring. Sleeping on a camp bed beneath the skylight
Full of drugs and gold—losing what you covet is not so hard if you no longer
See it. I won't ask what you've duly erased, I have no memory of the past eleven years
With regret, we recoil without the slightest palpitation.

The February deer, the winter-blue. The every other sunrise blunted.
The daughter says you drink, you like the American liquor, you comb your hair back, slick;
Our life receded at a speed of knots, every day I wonder who you are, strange—
I have nothing to carry. There is nothing in that palace except light.

My Telepathic Phonometrician

But if you are a scar—I am—you can't—
Worry me with body parts. Not even without
Journeys—I'm always surprised when I have
No idea. It's not supposed to be that way I am
Supposed to see it coming. Tasked with that—
Roaming—with the resemblance of something
Decapitated, but not quite—

     Baby I bring you the ghost's head. It's
Not supposed to be very revealing. Of anything—
The opposite, in fact. I should be transparent,
Like a shadow on a white chalk path in the morning.

*

She'd been decapitated indeed

*

I was first held at gunpoint aged fourteen.
It didn't seem a big deal down the Mercer Road.
Something about it was real but then
Something else was liminally foreign. When I
Didn't react they let me hold the gun,
Yes I was tempted to turn it on someone.
And yes, I remember his gold teeth. And the
Schoolgirl they had me fumble with
To *Siamese Dream*, with school ties, all legs
On a warm bed, beneath a window
In the summertime.

*

If we gather up all the things that are not that bad, nor *as bad as* something else
We are very dim philosophers.
                                              If it's not as bad as something worse
Is it better than a clenched fist. In the sun, bunched.

I was pleased to describe how she shuddered beneath the awning.
She shuddered like the abattoir pigs.
                                            How do you
Live with yourself? Is it just about as easy as this?

*

If I say you are qualified to judge
Perhaps I am also telling myself.
About God—in an acid trip He
Taught me a song. Diazepam
Mellowed it out to a hum
Caught on a puff of opium
In an organised-crime-run dress shop.
A man who looked like F. Zappa
Forgot to charge each day
I huffed away, sleeping with my head
On the shoulder of a militant biker.

*

Jade and I shaved our heads
So we could go to where my mother worked
And embarrass all her colleagues.
Instead they rubbed our stubbly heads
And suggested various hats
And curated our newly punked looks
And it was horrific.

We learnt to look toward the sun
When we were stoned, as though it helped
Anyone. We came home with grass stains
Rubbed in. No one asked. We puked
Down the front of my house
When the sun rose, to a metal anthem
And found it hilarious.

We saved baby birds and became
Adept arsonists. When a story ends—
Don't you feel sad. If no one knows
What happens next the thread is axed.
And she doesn't come home now or
Anytime, back. Lifts the baby, purrs. There is
No baby. Look, bunny—all gone.

*

Violence can't last forever by its own inhibited design.

*

Turn the music up until the speakers pop
So no one has to listen to the Luciferous papa

But I wanted to be witnessed most
So I hung out of the windowpane half-dressed

Waving at men falling out of the clubs
Listening to Snoop Dogg smoking chronic

Not everything was always long ago
Some things happen all the time

Like me now—here, listening
To the motherfucking electric fan

Fever peaking over the equatorial plane
And you as ever squeezing my vein

I'm all wet juice and no hot melon
With a cagey rind like paravane

*

Bravery happens in silence.

*

My cat Frank was fucking my leg when I woke
That isn't a joke. I rolled over and rolled my eyes
The sky was damp and grainy with tears.
        And I wished your face were next to mine
        Amused. I said I was amused
        When I heard her voice but
        When I saw her face I
        Wanted to rip her neck open
        With my paltry row of teeth.

I told my son if cats were very big they would
Eat us. They wouldn't hump our legs.

*

Erik Satie's piano
Cracked lips

You're making me honest
Don't hold back

Stiff legs
Raw shins

Ribcage birthmarks
Here he comes

*

Haloed now by a daylight moon
I write from my bed tummy to tummy
With a warm fuzz. A body

Wriggles. I cannot feel you.
Forty-eight-hour shakes. My dad calls
To talk about serial killings.

But not rapes. I buy a driver's license
And scout for rooms. I imagine you
Wish I were with you now.

Not in body—I have other powers.
I can rise above myself with my eyes closed
And watch myself having nightmares.

V.A. Fogg

The surgeon says *don't make me go back*
To the hospital. I stare him down and say *You?*
Man, you have a choice. I say *disappointment*
Is a chronic disease. I've seen it
All the time. He had the very same eyes,
Colour of his scrubs. White mask,
blue light, metal sharps. Us.

The sour smell comes in waves.
I didn't leave your side. And I was here,
Right here. All the time, while
You were scared, and finnicky,
And weak-brained. *This unseen trauma,*
I said. *It's got to come out sometime.*
I pricked my thumb with the scalpel

To show it's better when it bleeds.
This way is best. With drugs and restraints.
I mopped the sweat off your face. I
Cut it all out. When you woke,
You stood up and walked through me.
I caught up and you walked through me
Again. You just kept walking right

Through. Like I wasn't really there.
Like I wasn't really necessary.
Like I'd spilled too much of myself—
Becoming as thin as your gown.
Close the door. Swinging like a saloon.
Out the window of your room
A cordoned-off ocean.

Oh Hell

    Never getting asleep. It's brazen and brutal ain't it darling. Ain't it fucking cruel my
    Darling. Aren't I just not good. Aren't I brilliant.

                                         Aren't you tired of it.
                                         Go to sleep.
                                         Well stop talking and I'll
                                         Go right off
                                         But I was sitting here thinking about it
                                         Darling and I thought to myself
                                         Christ she's just not that good
                                         No I'm not that good
                                         Are you?

*

We had a societal problem. We had an insulation problem.
We had a bed problem. We ate dried strawberries in the bed.

And when you punched me on the ass right on the bone that meets
My body to my leg—I pretended not to be shocked. And I suppose

I wasn't all that shocked; because I've been hiding the pain I'm in
All my years. This is one for the feminists. This is one for the

Calvinists. This is one for the fingertips, where I touched you, you explained—
These erogenous zones are the most vulnerable places—the places

If we were animals that predators would devour first. I looked at the two
Blue chips of eyes in your head and receded within an epileptic seizure.

*

There are wild strawberries in the garden my lovely sweet
There are strawberries and there are sanitary pads and an old fridge

We disinfect the buckets and we crawl on our hands
We eat Bolognese sauce and dance to old jazz bands

*

In the dry grasses crickets climbed my legs to the hilt and I stung my calves on the nettles
I paraded my mettle.
                      Some daisies are big and some are small and Jim liked pansies.
                      I like geraniums. We shelled peas and built human-sized nests
                      With his shirt off he baked like polenta all gold and military

I said Jim it's ok to go off now it's okay to die no one's here but me it's a good time to go.
It's a good time to go isn't it Jim?

*

But when I thought you were the most intense object I'd ever looked at
Perhaps the night was draining the rest of the audience or perhaps
I thought you were too intense to be looked at by an object like me.

Someone climbed onto a table with their breasts out. Sagging into skin
Like old hands. It was terribly embarrassing. She's since become famous.
I lie in a cornfield and imagine I'm a rattlesnake looking for mice.

*

Out of a suitcase, not sure of anything at all. If I could just
Match the dicks to the faces I'd make more sense of bodily phenomena
But as it is there are simply seas and oceans and hard drives full of dicks—

Hard dicks, squashy dicks. Lord I'm so tired I just.
        You're Greek and you want to boss me about. You're livid
           And you want to pay a lout fifty pounds to work me over.

        I'm tired and you're annoyed and I'm sexy and you're three-legged.
        I'm bleeding from many places and no man enjoys wearing condoms
        And no man enjoys pain derived in isolation from his potent thrusting.

Lord, I'm so bored. My suitcase is on its dead legs. My body sighs unexplored.
I made a packet today mopping up the excess mourning. I carried myself light
And the threshold was met inexpensively, unexpansive. Love, stay put.

*

Radial it comes through the scapulae to the high point of the scalp;
I get electrical on heat. Baby at the window, tap tap tap—come back
When I'm more fortunate.
                            Of course I am not sorry. You
Did me a railroading of harm. You'd turn the keys in the ignition and start
Screaming. I was so ashamed I couldn't tell anyone I was afraid to be driven
Home.

*

Please let me in I'm only a spoon in your mouth I'm
Not trying to damage your teeth your dogtooth it's
All the lambs bleating mercilessly and the Tosca poured over—

Me? I'm sorry I was just about to be magnificent right then and
You got me so down. In the long grasses the ticks inject you in
The forge the flies nibble your juiciness. You can't win honey no.

But there is an entrance such an entrance to a cornfield you must
Enter me now. Is it possible to avoid lying down right in this stewing
Hodgepodge of the posh and no honey no one is nearly as interesting

Not now they have us doubled. I am not a gem you think too—
It is yes it is possible to live in this ruthless way it's the way of the living
The still alive after all. After all. Why would I love you when you have nothing

But queries. Dot said leave the teabag in said it was too damned hot.
My hair fell out all over the ceramics and I pressed my hand to my brow—
Got beaten. If it helps you can imagine that I miss you very much.

*

And you were dying there just momentarily. Then in a moment.
You were there, dying, and it took so long you rattled and gurgled yourself up.

When you squeezed my hand I knew you were at last come back to yourself.
I put the little sponge back in the drinking cup. I wiped your slackened mouth.

*

If you're afraid of dying my darling you are missing right out.
                                                            Peril is
Desperately important.
                    It is and I never avoid it. Sometimes I even undress
And run after it.
                Like I did when I saw you yes you are right and look at how that
Ended.

*

Beyond the green dress parade and you in a shirt and tie not a pat of fat on you and white—
Did we shuffle close? I think we touched hips and maybe you put an arm around me but
You were drunk, no? I was speeding my tits off on bad coke. Doesn't matter, these things are
Irrelevant. I decided I was off limits to anything with a literary agent. I decided I was lost
To my affaire with sensation.

                              I know it was a hot night—the devil had a stunning array
Of patchwork. He made the sky into a patchwork something or other—he crocheted the town.

Imagine if we'd not been drowned and we'd found a place to fall asleep together; oh, how I needed
Sleep. In the morning I cried and then someone played Avro Pärt and I decided to commit suicide.
Well it's not very romantic is it my love. Chemicals do that in abundance. I needed the oxytocin
You get from pressing a chest to a chest or skin to a hand or a face to a thigh, I don't know.
Perhaps we'd still be lovers now.
                                   You should see the spiders in this place—the moths—
The giant's eyelids in the bathroom towels. I am only almost-good. You are indeliberate.

*

He sneezed right into my eye wah-shoo.
I had an intolerable dose of déjà vu.

The porcelain turtle on the wall and the
Seahorse they are faceless and cracked.

I frightened a pheasant right out of its nest.
I haven't felt sexual anguish in days.

Not even for you. Messages come at midnight.
Men don't have any self-control you know. No

They don't and I don't mind that. I'm
Utterly benevolent in love on perfect overdrive.

*

No I don't love you.
You know it. You don't love

Anyone.
>	It doesn't matter if I love you
>	You wouldn't love me if I loved you.
>	You shouldn't.

*

Soundbites exploring the Cotswolds for the first time. Rustic.
Old-style. Circumcised. Appley. God didn't meet me, M. Not
This time. He's busy with the dead and dying.

I should never have gotten into that car. I wouldn't
Remember anything about it except it was black and tired.
When I reached the Travelodge I sighed *fuck me Jesus* at reception.

The man behind the desk gulped hard.

Golden Palaces

We will fly to the Palace of Knossos and have
Nothing in the world left to cry about. Your gold

Spine will lie in the sand and be warmed while the sky
Swirls in a spell to give me to your arms at once.

Where are you now. The room is very small, and the hours
Slot into place and vanish. I went all over everywhere

Trying to find something to make me—I was shrinking
And now the size of us. I would like it all to be white

And sparkling. The air white, the sea white, the sky
Transparent and our bodies sat inside the white cloud

Of white knowing and not even see the whites
Of your eyes just the peeling heart and the sunshine

In it. But you can't make these things. You can't
Arrive. But I want horses and a beach made out of

Peachskins and cherry blossoms and a sad-faced clown
Worrying about us and seals slapping their tails and

Laughter whooping all around the globe til it comes back
And smacks us. My teeth are set because they would bite

You very much. I will need something to eat. We will
Not need to sleep ever again I have a plan. Spiriting me

Will take a lot of energy and love will want me pretty
Or nevermind. I'm full of pear juice. My mother said

I grew from an appleseed, in a linen shroud. I had
Twelve big dreams in the womb. I had seven more

Just last night. I had three children all with the same name.
I had a heart like an ark full of pairs of animals;

They made such a lot of noise wanting to get out of there.
But what will happen will there be a sadness, a big torment

Yes there will and there will be flying things and stars. But
Will there be blood and dirt and toothache. Those too,

Because we have bodies. But will there be a good thing,
A pure good thing at the heart of it. There will if you can

Take up in a rush of hurricane and set yourself down
And not fall into the Earth or disappear again.

Caroline

'Time recedes with a fatal drop.' — FLEETWOOD MAC, 'Caroline'

Teeth took a while to grow back in—
I fell asleep under the drill hugging the obelisk.
Things hurt more when you are loved than when
You're hated. And then I was feared.
I put the bones all neatly at your door.
I labelled them all so you'd recognise they
Were yours. I spilled

Muesli on the keyboard and the machine
Chewed up my card and my husband
Changed his number. I remembered
I hadn't slept and had a bruise like a mouth
On my face. All I know is that you kept saying
You were going, and you didn't go.
I paid the bill for your champagne.

I walked to the jazz club in a blanket
In the snow. I tipped the scorpions
Out of our shoes in the morning. I tried
To walk everywhere so to avoid more gazes.
The waiter said he'd wrap the leftovers
So I could take them home. I need
One hundred pounds. A measly, limpid

One hundred in notes. One hundred
And the IOU keeps growing. And then
They know where you live because they
Follow you. You have to start calling
Further and further out until
One day you're in Birmingham,
Next day you're in Brixton.

Monday nights there's no one to call.
The White Goddess laughs through your window
And the voile blinds shake. The old men
Ride around all night on penny farthings.
You reply and tell him it's a date—
But both know it really isn't. The Giacometti
On the wall has faded badly in the sun.

Blackout # 57 w/ Snow Drift and Premature Meteorite Burst

So Telamon, I woke and drilled a hole in the wall ahead of myself as a lookout.
The temporary porthole grew iconic fur and edged me over a blue velvet chide—
Snow wriggled in the suburban dawn with no thing pure or white
Or particularly 'drifting'; neither through movement nor in support of any circumference reached towards;
Slept under an armpit like a pheromone cloud and wished sublime damnation upon us.

Vixen one living in a shelter of shelf life, half-life and things you can turn
Off and on; electric fails due to tripwire, Poor Romanticism—
Falling on laurel upon laurel until all I can say is I never ate out
Of any hand, and they fed me the idea I was a suck-up or siamese for poverty porn.
No more, we go to Mass in our head.

Temptation is nothing until it solidifies through language, carcass or ash;
If there's no word for the ingested or wanted object then it meets your tread.
Give it words like NEED or JUT and acquire its taste with great dedication; love
I'm still addicted. Lean through the crack in the dream he had and feel fur against
My cheek. A partition opens in which I slur words, drop-out to drift or roll downwards;

Pigeon-first towards an indescribable face of a dream, a face of holes,
Orifices, assholes—these white sheets don't release when born in a third-world peace protest; I;
White dust. The golden stuff in liquorice paper with infinite PH value,
Makes me so nice. Can't trace me now; over the muff of Pendle, crossbow to sturdy
Aimed headwards, firedrill and more fire still as I lay naked leaching Blackburn of fossil fuel—

Sleep right there and don't crawl, poor light or dud.
Wearing white if I can or must as though it is meaningful to have ditched the devastating black-
Satin zip-up peep-hole bodice with cherry-topped ice buns on a mountain of dug-grave;
I eat out, my saliva moistens the mouth that no longer
Senses a distance between love and hunger or between you and here or

Between there and the core of the earth as it apparently hums.
Dearest leper of mine, no one else goes all that far but if it's not felt,

All the better. Dreamt of you and a cricket bat, cider with vodka is not that helpful;
Brookside Close home with terrorist undertones, flora and fauna pushed to the ditches
And the roads. Smoke to reach the end of the street then turn to a tread

And deepen on contact with grounds for divorce being that they are impossible
To ascertain. Can't you just tell the judge you despise me for being clever.
Slide down the gorge in white cowboy boots and feet too big to be a girly-pie.
My mother's face churns in the basin. All forbidden things unseen though still constituting
Five hundred percent of my psycho-geographical make-up.

I see a bag on the ground I pick it up. Doctor Ray warns me pain relief is addictive.
Little white coke-break, haven't seen strange in a wee little while. I take things seriously, sure.
The first thing I bought with the literary award was a pink dildo, which, on arrival
Was too big to use. Second thing I bought was ten grams of coke. Third was smack
And fourth was Bacofoil Original. There was a new pen, but that I stole.

When I get caught shoplifting I pretend I'm retarded, a little too well.
You can achieve anything at all if you couldn't care less about it. Ah, my girl.
Freeze-dipping swells over the sunk-belly whilst all birds migrate the fuck out of England.
We're together now, the ley lines writhe between us and all x's mark forgettable hotspots.
All things have a memory, even my pins and my needles.

You're a hole in space, sir; an anomaly, if you will; I can see
Through Time from this lookout in thine sugar-encrusted boudoir you are stuck.
Whiskered, etc, amen and thus I wrote what you told me to that time
I hyperventilated down the phone with too much drilling going on
And here I am, caryatid, and knee deep in cheap Taiwanese lace.

Haint Blue

The whole town has the pox. Annesie comes with a plate of food,
A cup of mango lassie; I'll love you even when you run to Monaco,
And I'll own even less than I have right now. There is
A train comes over this way, it begins South and moves through the lowlands,
The marshes and ditches that couple went killing for fun, it runs
From here all the way to the Highlands. If it did, would you come?

At Loch Ness with that too-young husband of mine, I tip-toed
In scarlet sandals between men in galoshes, every fist I saw was octopus red.
I tried to do different things in bed, things newer than fruit and sweeter
Than ponies roaming in the dew in the newly barren woods with their rotten hooves.
Winter was not a time then, it was a discovery. There was so little to eat
I forgot taste. I had the pills in the pillbox to treat me fine.

Pink champagne, and I climbed a mountain in black stockings;
I didn't know how to pack. Sometime there was a seed or an egg,
There was a cloud and a beginning. Pillars. It depends what time means to you.
Have you thought of what is on top of us? Not merely on top
Or above but way over our heads? I think you're there, not haint but gold,
In a striped suit milking a fat cow for cream, dipping your fingers in it.

Yes, the grass when I was very young was different. Suns crept up on me,
The world was all treasure. If I was cold so was the devil. If I was sick
The devil crept up. Haints were a comfort in the wide white room, the twin bed empty
Of a sister. I told the girl I lost her brother in the womb, but he was born,
In a way. She'd been leaving out toys for years, ponies, trying to learn
His name. It's better sometimes not to have one. My name

Only sounds like my name to one person. I just didn't want
More time. When I fell asleep on the beach on Mallorca and rose
To a language I couldn't comprehend, burned like mad I stung like Bethulia,
I wanted your head. So stoned in fair Italy I might have been dead,

And nobody could teach me to drive. In a dream last night my husband says
He is my father. Like my father. He's nothing like my father.

He is more muscular, he drives a car full of brats, he is Orpheus
If Orpheus grew up soulless, he is still mine. I can't say what's on my mind
For the censors are making their play for Monaco, and I'm sweeping the lawn
In my jejune dress, picking up the broken pegs, the notches of the spine.
There is something chemically wrong. I break you into parts to make some sense;
Milk cow, violets, sand dunes, lakesides, Degas; haints.

Rhett Butler

Always I'd be dragging a skirt
Made of old curtains through
A river pissing blood, all
Torn up. Summer used to be
High yellow. And we never got to eat
Butter. Sometimes some strange
Kinds of pink tinned meat
Eaten from a wrapper on the way
Home, thirsty and wandering—
Thinking, going flowerpicking
On your own. Imagining Rhett
Butler as the father not the junkie
Father the lover the one delayed—
Smiling like a slapped ass,
Handing me the lunchbox,
Sitting on the doorstep of a
Repossessed terraced house sleeping
Fine behind the sleep factory gnawing
Its teeth through on my dreams,
Winding the dial over and over,
Greensleeves and stuffed doll shadows—
Slumped by the windowsill where I sit
To get cool and wait for Rhett.
Locked in past seven at night for the
Falling, when the sky has a shiner
Or worse. Sat on the ironwrought steps
Counting white butterflies shivering, many
Scarlet and rosepetal, cough candy so
Very nice if I ask him. And
A hoe-down and a ball where the
Frogspawn stinks in the puddle there of
Burnt amphibians—the sun too hot and
The ferrets and the white mice living their lives

Out in the coal scuttle. Ladybugs dancing about
Our bitten legs. When my sister
Played with boys she got her hand all
Cut up. I dressed it with my best
Lace socks. She bit me twenty-two
Times. Pink and blue chalk hopscotch.
The scary green light like a holographic
In the forest past the big road one hundred
Miles long and it can take you home,
But there's no way of going. Blinking in
The phonebox in the midsummer rain
And he drives to visit me, Rhett,
With his hay-smelling baby rodents and these
Ill-gotten treasures. Rhett at Sunset. Rhett
Driving the Milk-Float. Rhett and me locked in
The damp Broom Cupboard. Fingers on the
Ivory phone where the numbers wind around,
Always go back to the start with a ring.
A leather wallet, and a catapult. I
Have it all in my jewellery box,
The musical ballerina with her spinning
Cut off head, my sister she gets angry about
Beautiful things. A rack of old knuckles,
For three billy goats. I rap my knuckles
On the bedhead when he closes his smoky
Eyes lays back all remorseful and
The friendly moon stops glowing
Just like that it stops radiating the light of the star
For just about the last honest hour of every night.

Bird-Watching

Counted fifteen dead birds on the lawn this morning waiting for the maggots to come.
I tried to see what the other writers evidently saw beyond the extinction hysterias and manifestos
But, it wasn't birds—there was nothing for me, no demiurge. My universe does not want to meet yours;
And whilst A-listers fly great distances to attend air travel protests, I ask myself
What a bird's-eye view of myself could mean whilst I'm buried or bored.

Don't you remember that summer when my broken skin would reflect all light and sound from the pounding?
The young have taken to bird-watching and anal sex. The state of Grace has gone unreplicated.
My stepfather accused me of destroying his marriage because I gave him a Ouija board
On his fifty-first birthday. I was taking so much acid at the time. Of course,
Who knows what supernatural things happen to us without our knowing.

From the garden pool I step on a frog, onto a needle, into a very deep sleep.
I sleep hard with the head of a bird, the coma is wild, I read about twenty-one years later
I died. I was a worm afraid of all things bird-related, which would be entirely obvious should you ever
Be that low in the ground. The Doctor told me he'd seen it too and asked me what I found—Sir,
The soil was terribly claggy and neutral and the subsequent flight into the arms of a man

I had no desire to love was just as bad. I broke up with him over the phone. I became extremely good
At writing. A period of incarceration as a psychotic post-coma patient led me to detain my body
With a complement of drugs. My friends were imagined. There were such tales reported of the birds
Who watched me squirm against the hands of physicians. They recorded all the swear words I said.
I whirred my index finger round in the air as though I knew what I was doing, to frighten them.

So now you're here what will you do with it? Your sight. Your lack of intuit. I always knew
There was something in me birds admired. The way they crashed into my windows on sight.
The way they nested in my bedclothes, nourished on bedbugs, danced on my fingertips.
My step-dad said I was allergic. Anaphylactic shock once killed me, I laid there whilst he prophesied,
'She's going to die.' It interested me to have this subjective viewpoint of the way I was objectified.

Now I do remember all the times I've been held down, pinned. But to even talk
Takes more cells than I can use these days. Yes, do stay in the city with your little sun hats and Jesus,

He loves you of course, far more than anyone else. I was always sensitive to my family's comedy
Depictions of me saving starlings and sparrows from certain death, spinning around with their
Delicate bodies in my open palms, spinning until they'd invariably fall out and die on the roadside.

I made epic contraptions to house spiders in, believing it better for them. Their skeletons seemed to
Vanish quite soon into a faint brown dust. I thought you knew what was best when you
Had me committed. I missed stealing ice lollies from the old man's sweet shop on bank holidays,
And having skin fall off in chunks from my face. It was the purgatory I deserved; I suppose.
It was easier existing in that windowless place. I just wish that you'd called.

Fatherland

He lay on his back in the deflated pool fully clothed t-shirt speckled in rain
Eyes closed all the world reduced to a single point in the sky. I made sandwiches
A headless bird with a single plume of blue tail feathers reclined beside him.
So far his father has said little but sent a photograph of his mother holding our son.
That we're dead and I'm alive means nothing. *The colour Blue seen in a dream.*

The sky he said is white through yellow to purple then pink and I squinted
A kestrel swerved across the arc of our land. The wind is belting the walls, I sweat here
Drifting about in the glade. I tell the daemon to try to recognise the sadness when it comes
Or it returns. My mother gave me twins and several learned songs I lay them in cots
And fasten their buttons. So much of my life has never belonged with me.

I told Betsy she had a brother who died in the womb beside her she used to play lonely
Games lonely long days unsure of what she missed, lonely horses. I was afraid of silence
Because of this—facing all—foetuses, abject lack of lure, my blue two selves, my greening irises.
But I found a prismatic tendency; I found I had it all there cooking in my own eyes.
When the child first took the camera he pointed it at the buttercups, he said he knew what to do

Though he'd never used a frame before. He knew nothing of Yellow or Green but shapes
Have enough vibrancy to make a life. The spectres are much clearer. I know if I don't see you
You're not there. I know I can't dance or make house but this brain! I know I have a certain
Lack of expression. My father he can't die again. Peeling the swabs off the bed; remember
When I was full of holes? You bathed me and rubbed my jerking legs. I wonder sometimes

If I stopped eating, if I stopped anything, what would come. I don't believe in hungriness.
The daughter I loved best was indecisive. She was against everything. Sometimes
I go into her room just to relive how it felt to be the purest source of love. Clean sheets,
Blue lights. The brother and she shared a bed it was like she'd remembered the lost boy. And Betty
Lost a baby too, and when she died we all were sleeping. I bought bourbon for the shock.

There's an overpass in my corpus callosum, I had such an idea! My memories of you could be
From any era. I've seen collapse, I know what will come. You'll be behind glass, perhaps all of it
Does happen backwards. Gasping for air is a kind of music, there is a terrible rhythm.
My legs pale blue stalks twitching out in front of me. Never afraid; what mettle it takes to succumb.
I will surround myself with more blue things before next June. Moses in his basket

In the reeds is how it all begins. Something wrathful, something warm. My hypergraphia
Persisted; there was a world saturated deep as Friedensreich's halcyon. I saw a lovely thing today
Beyond the balloons and the crotchets—beyond colour. My son, my son.

White Mist

    It wasn't a red mist it was white.
        It was holocaust white.
    Slowboiled,
    I got pissed on it.
        Filled my heart
    Licked my gums.

*

Master I'm enraged and I'm thinking of you chewing on my inner thighs
I want to be able to kill people with my thighs thighs thighs.
My honey hole—no. West side of town is all drive-bys and scumlickers.
This life has shut me up. No one lives—I want another. I applied before anyone—
I said god I want to live on an island or where they have very loose gun laws.
Les is in a hole now. He did all the sex things. He did all of them.
Holy fucking hell.

*

I have bones in my legs you know. You have too.
You have bones and femurs and arm-bones and neck-bones
And a hyoid bone and a skull and two ankles. You have things
Growing up out of you. Everyone does. Nothing I can kiss.

*

To be destroyed in the vent of extraordinary carnage
My surreptitious one. Give me your palm and your tearducts
While I fawn over apocalyptic visions and you saying nothing.

Something to weight the eyes draw the dilating pupils out
If not you then. I put my pink face in love up to the neckline,
Cascade all over. Untouching, listless, I pore; helpless—

Squirrel in an elm tree spitting on my hair. This punk up high
Watching me forage, slurping Mountain Dew. Somewhere else
Sits the sky, wondering why it is what it appears to be—

Blue, old and see-through. Last night in hot water I found you.
I take more than I need you say *sure*. Don't mean it. Riding shotgun—
Olympian, taut, moreover—made you swim. Look—

I won't see you tomorrow. No. Or any other day soon.
Soon is relative, as is coupling. Feed it—blow it—exhume—
I am low-down, I am edged-in. Sensitised to your *glowing*.

And they want documents, pages, evidence. They want
Me to blow over. Fuming, I hand over my dignity and haul ass,
Trying to fall over my failings. When they call me up

I must be emotionless, like I am every time they call.

*

No Führer I don't know his name. I know his face.
I know his stomach and his arms. I know his hair
And his eyes. He knows my anus. He is not really a valid person.
     He is not really a person at all.

You want to make him be a person, I understand.
He doesn't know anything. He's scraped off the door. You could
Feed him for years and still he would not get bigger—
     Care if I lived or died that night.

I roll over and face the wall and kick. I can see where
The blood ran. I can see me with my bent arm.
I can hear the bone crack.

*

We start out the days with love. We conjure one another loveably.
We shiver under the lure of one another. We fail to examine.

I want you to know I am living—like the dead live hopefully
In the mind. I was close to forgetting, then you showed.

The worst thing I ever did—is hard to decide.
The best thing—impossible to imagine or decipher.

We're real yes but the world isn't. Darling you blink
And my face slams shut. And I only want you to own me.

*

Telling geese to fuck off back to Canada

*

He's extremely pretty and he asked me to devour his loneliness in one bite.
He said he would try to avoid saying things that were trite.
He's young and he's sweet and his blood tastes like marbles.
He does not know when I am this mad my hair falls out.
He doesn't know what pain that makes you black out feels like.
He will never, ever be able to see me not even if I'm twenty-two feet.
I want to pet him and apologise for it.

*

Because I could have just one drink.
They carry the boy away with the deftness of saints.
I don't know how when they're finitely stoned; strychnine white.
One summer I bought my son a blue kite.

But the lad by the church he's dead as.
There is always something biblical about it—dying junkies
With snaky legs. Children shrunken up into their selves.
I'm running to be different. A different kind of bait.

I tot up and memorise the things I hate.

*

Stomping along the canal I realise I can cry with white-hot rage.
I have twenty-eight epiphanies a day these days.

*

There was an angel riding on my back last night. I winked at her.
I winked at Danny without thinking about it. I clock all the exits.

I want to inadvertently display all my secrets. I want the boys to pick me up.
I want to steal a car tonight and drive over. I want to ram-raid a bank.

There is a memory to this place. The roads are crispy with it. They fry.
My feet hit the pavements and my shins shatter and all I can do is cry.

But this would not stop me, ever. You know that. What if I am right.
What if you scoop me up with one paw and I never get over it.

Once I got all I needed from sunlight. I played in the splintery back street
I didn't want to ask for anything because I knew I couldn't have it.

*

Freedom is a thought process we all play about with.

*

You've been playing with me.
I'm tired.

*

Shush.

*

Why don't you just break my legs
And put me in a chair
And train my gaze on the ocean floor.

Master I can't do this anymore.
I can't go on.
Words keep clinging to my knees.

I'm begging.

*

To be tied up and kept in the shed—
Gagged, of course—mutilated—
In an isolated place—you have to think—
It can't be local—no and not too cold—

I would be happy, yes. I would be enslaved.
I want it all out of my hands. We are
Trapped. A collar would be nice.
And a postcard too.

I'll sit on my hands. I'll sleep.

I'll lose all my names and my eyesight.
I won't ask where everyone has gone
Because everyone has left.
I'll wear your teeth like lockets
Around my collarbone—in this
Misanthropic fantasia—where I am kept
Like a toy. Because I am a toy.

Because wouldn't it be nice to be
Nothing more than a toy?
To have zero control, and no purpose
But making you feel like a God

In your running tights. Yes.
It's nice to have these sufferable feelings
Sometimes. But where can you buy
All of that rope?

*

Honestly, I don't think I can. I am a witch my dearest.
I can disappear myself. But I can't make you come home.
Not from here. Not in my bluewhite bitchskin.

*

Me and Esmeralda used to canter through the north fields
Socked in my velvet boots.
         She was a big girl. The biggest.
     When I fell she got hoarse with annoyance.

Have the air cutting through my face. My face open in the sky.
I always wanted to die.

And then I died and it was no fun.
When you die you can't even tell anyone.

No you cannot. Do you understand what it means to have to wake up?
Well it was a great shock I can explain.
I thought you were into it. You wore me,
Like a suit. And I bolted without you, any of you.

*

I promise
This is it
This is wanted
And furthermore
Delusions are boring
Stories are telling
Minds get sore and
Dicks get hard

I went to war
Today I went hunting
I was in the thicket
In a hairshirt
Collecting wood
For the pyre
When you messaged
Oh my god I said
Holy fuck
And
Damn

Where are you
Situated in time
Telling god tales
I got spanked
When I was insolent
The impressions were welted
I sucked my thumbs
In my twenties
No shit
I lived hard

Sad and all open
Sad and all opened up
You peer into my cavity
I bubble with excitement
But I do not breathe
And you do not fill it
With all this talk
That's all I am
Even to you
Bloodsweat in the afternoon
Entirely unknown

*

Goaded and railroaded
A train suicide
Splayed eagerly in millennial red

*

The master and his emissary

For tea on the eleventh
I fuck on the Sabbath
The rest is on you

*

The middle of June my petit-déjeuner doesn't exist
It's not in any diaries the world over
Ask my mum
Ask Satan
Lunchdates
Bedmates

*

Why won't you take me away in your broken car
And stroke my dark hair while I'm sleeping is it
Really so hard to be kind. Will spacetime fracture
Will the seas become slime will my skin still fizz
When I read your name. Am I gone now darling.
It was a catastrophic catastrophe.
Our four legs buckle at the same time.
I go to church and ask god to fuck me.
I go flying over rooftops licking my lips.
My god have you been actually crying.
My cells roll happily down the Styx
Screaming freedom and arrivederci
In a round. There is no spell to
Gather me up
Your arms are shored
Your eyes are tired
Your bed is made
I'm very bored.

Slingers

                      All that jaw in your face. Jaundice
                      I thought was all the orange juice.
                      We liked our vodka with it & Melleril,
                      A little heroin and microwavable burgers.
                      No one should die shivering like that
                      At least a fairly warm death or
                      I don't know. When you know you are
                      About to die violently and there's
                      No way out your body floods your brain
                      With so much dopamine
                      You can't feel a thing. Want to know
                      How I know that?

Apple Rain

What makes you so sure, he says. As though all past is a future discovery.
I'm not sure that I am truly apart. I just know there is silence.
Three worlds between which I carried myself. Little swollen stars and planets
Moving apart too fast to record them. In the middle a black hole spews
But does not eat—it's nonsense. How can you be sure.

Lay out for me all those things you know. Do you absolutely know them.
Ask questions without inflection. In that hut the dog was driven mad
By the constant bleating of sheep. I took him home, stayed gone.
You slept by the sea. No one called for weeks. I thought I was saved;
But distance is the illusion of being forgotten, being apart, and it's wearing.

To know that we are separate yet to see where we conjoin; not to want the bones
Crammed in and dragged along even when they're broken. I could
Kill you for mercy in your sleep if it came to that. I was not able
To watch you suffer. Perhaps this is an unnerving thought—I wasn't to know.
What I can do and what I did are very different.

And she said she will call so I begin to pick up and all they want is money; so much
Money I cannot think. Eventually I am destined to unplug the phone.
Would you not respond. Did I do anything shameful behind the deluge, in the dark hotel.
I explain when the bluebells come underfoot and when they wilt,
I know when the cherry blossom begins to make me divulge my secret.

I know when the rain is minutes from falling, I can tell you where the heart is
Pointing to the place. I can tell you when your pulse is ragged and how many years
You have left. All of these things you must not want to know.
I stitched my own wounds, I am made for these times. Still these
People don't see what's coming. Me and my junkie picked those crab apples late;

We swung the boughs lazily and gathered them up at the roadside whilst businessmen
Avoided us. Dirty men would give us free jerk chicken at closing. I would
Stay awake just knowing things. My body indented into so many mattresses,

Between them all I was a bead of sweat, perhaps remembered. Good homes are not echoic.
Won't you listen to me? As I stood there airless and tense

A catalogue of my own failures, she perched on the velour Chesterfield and made light.
I had every defence memorised. I had all of the reasons and sense, but
No one to ask, no witness. I recalled the young officer, I never forget;
Standing in court, hand on a bible, heaving with sobs, your mother howling,
Everything the coroner found laid out. I was late because

I was smoking on the courthouse steps. Not because I killed or because I couldn't look.
What I'd already seen was tantamount to horror. I started buying lollipops
Every day. Cherry, cola. When my daughter put ham in the DVD player I smiled.
I placed all the photographs I ever took in a skip on the outskirts of town.
I saved several lives and continued to flounder, calling dead numbers

Under a willow tree aged to a husk. Do you think these things last?
Our subjective realities are inherently different, how could we love?
How can you stay in that audience after the star of the show is carried off? Every night
There is nothing left. So many nights I pretend it is morning. My thoughts
Shave hours off. The wind carries a call to prayer.

The small boy with black hair covering his eyes taps on my window each day.
The cat's whiskers twitch, I draw the curtains on waking. Things really happened
When she was here. Apples rained down on Accrington in the summer of '83,
Some people are still bruised. It was a drop of blood on my shoe that brought me round,
It was vile and sad that day. I called your mother. I had to throw the shoes away.

Of all the places to haunt. I was marooned as a runaway, I don't know
About you. I used to draw every face I adored. Totems; Ida's sundial, the river deer, the roasted
Flowers. Too many souls trying to disappear. The lower tier of the atmosphere
Prevents us bleeding into space. I think sometimes of all the things I'd help you see,
But then I close my eyes. You are all doing so well.

Acknowledgements

This book is a window into a huge body of my work written over the past seven years. In that time I could not have survived without the love, support and assistance of all of the following organisations and individuals:

I would like to thank The Royal Literary Fund and the Society of Authors for their financial assistance in times of hardship. Spires, a South East London charity for the homeless gave me much needed assistance and support as did the Deptford 999 club, CGL Lewisham and Sparks Blackburn. Thank you to Penned in the Margins and Tom Chivers for supporting me and publishing my first three collections. A very special thank you to my confidante, Anne Worthington, for several years of life-saving support and insight to which I am forever indebted.

Much admiration and respect to Donald Winchester at Watson, Little for supporting this project.

Unending gratitude for the following beautiful souls for helping me up when I was at the very bottom: Nicholas Lezard, Jess Mookherjee, Cath Nichols, Giles Turnbull, Thomas Smith, Siegfried Baber, David Ashford, Andrea Clarke, Dean Rhetoric, Jarred, Ollie Yarrow, Vg Lee and Daniel & Emily Brenchi-Sluman.

Love and deepest admiration forever goes out to Mark Waldron, Danny Moran, Michael Wyndham, Tom Bland, Stevie Kilgour, Bobby Parker, Bonnie Hansell, Luke Kennard, Gemma Lovell, Dai George, Rishi Dastidar, Matthew Caley.

Bless you Robbie Grounds, for sticking with me through the impossible. And thank you Jos for having faith in me all these years.

Everything I write is in some way for Jade Charmaine Gedling, who has been gone twenty years and yet I can still see, hear and smell her as though she was just right in front of me. She is always loved.

Stephen Pickles, you were a truly great man and mentor, and I miss you deeply.

Over the years I've met so many writers, made so many friends and shared many ideas and drafts with truly brilliant writers and artists who have taught me a great deal about life and love, as well as writing. People come and go, all things must change, but there are many who will stay in my thoughts, and whose work I will turn to again and again.

Love and light to Jamie, for seeing it through with me.

Praise for *Exposure / Ideal Palace*

"I've just heard a sound: it's every 'How to Write Poetry' website in the world, crashing. To try to get at the scale, scope and sustained intensity of Melissa Lee-Houghton's *Exposure / Ideal Palace*; you'd have to think De Sade's inexhaustible erotic scatology; or imagine Captain Beefheart following up *Trout Mask Replica* with a quadruple album. Apart from anything else everyone is going to have to do some serious reading; not skimming, or scanning, scrolling or grazing the surface. Forget tired analogies with Confessionalism, always a (relatively tame) quasi-Symbolist practice. Think Dominique Aury or George Bataille or Proust, but the Proust who reputedly stuck pins in rats in order to orgasm, rather than the elegant prose-stylist (though there's elegance and 'prose' here too). But keep the tidal pull of all these. And just as you're about to proclaim your own *'There are the Alps, fools!'* moment, you're hit by elegant? / meta-elegant? / elegant? poems that wind in and around (very tangentially) Le Palais Idéal du Facteur Cheval. The last poet, I seem to recall, who used this trigger-point was late modernist Ronald Johnson in his long poem *Ark*. Your own re-adjusted preconceptions (now vibrating at overdose-high-orgasm-hangover-come-down level simultaneously) will have to be further re-adjusted. Meanwhile, these 'two-books-in-one' continue to outstare and metabolically adjust each other. Even if you find you hate it, you'll still be secretly sick with jealousy. It's a thing: a brutal and wildly beautiful 'self-portrait' in its own entire landscape, that still can't contain itself or be 'stood back from', or rivalled. Utterly vital."
MATTHEW CALEY · author of *Apparently* and *Rake*

"The welding of pleasure to rage in these poems makes the violent daily gaze and the rotten soul of capital jump out of its shit-scared skin. But *Exposure / Ideal Palace* is not an Idealist project, rather detailing the stains—the skin hanging on, addicted maybe, but also connected, like how each of the poems connects singularly to the book as a whole: 'a sunset held timidly in place'. Melissa Lee-Houghton's epic, her glam materialist poetics, is 'beyond the good/bad dichotomy' and so this book is pedagogical, as in 'don't dictator me' and don't forget to desire, to feel. Something shockingly difficult to do today, so we need this, ie. this book is necessary, why be surprised that it is joyful too?" **REBECCA CLOSE** · translator and author of *Valid, Virtual, Vegetable Reality*

"Melissa Lee-Houghton's *Exposure / Ideal Palace* is 'a fever of defiance'. These poems are a blazing account of the erotic splendour, despair and violence of living, of how joy can be found even though there's a 'bone lodged in the throat' of your life. Lee-Houghton's senses 'touch on all things'. The result is a book that leaves you reeling with 'histamines and bliss', your own senses simultaneously agitated and soothed."
AMY KEY · author of *Arrangements in Blue* and *Isn't Forever*

"'Just how immediate can a poem be?', asks Melissa Lee-Houghton in this startling, visceral new collection. Well, it just can't be any less immediate than what you'll read here—words that don't describe pain and love and grief and flesh but that are all those things in themselves—we are not reading about something here because Lee-Houghton manages through the terrifying beauty of her poetry to get rid of the 'about'. There's no barrier between the poems and their subject matter, which gives these works a kinship to the Metaphysical poetry of the past, but with added tramadol, heroin and pregabalin." **DARIAN LEADERY** · author of *What is Madness*, *Strictly Bipolar* and *Sexuality, Suffering & Satisfaction*

"With its long lines and its hard joy, with its defiance in the face of darkness, *Exposure / Ideal Palace* is Melissa Lee-Houghton's song of herself. In going that far down into the dark it somehow flies. Because these poems do seem to emerge from a few layers further underground than other poems, and on the way up they get pushed through fewer filters. The book is full of extraordinary ideas and humour, the drugs look 'so pretty and secular', or 'Look at this mouth, does it look like a safe place to keep a fantasy'. And, as another poem says, 'who would want to lie next to me? No one sleeps next to the ravine, do they'. But it turns out, being next to that ravine is an exhilarating place to be." **MARK WALDRON** · author of *A Straight up Giant* and *Meanwhile, Trees*

"Visceral, fraught and intoxicated, Lee-Houghton's poetry sheds light on a hardscrabble existence, a psychic descent into turmoil and disintegration. This is fearless writing, one reporting from the frontline of homelessness, addiction and obsessive love." **ADELLE STRIPE** · author of *Ten Thousand Apologies* and *Black Teeth & a Brilliant Smile*

"These are extraordinary poems. *Exposure / Ideal Palace* is at once sprawling and controlled. This collection is unending and capacious, with long lines that form chains of images and ideas, piling up. This is a unique, formally bold meditation on what it is to write, 'making life out of calamity'." **FRANCESCA BRATTON** · author of *Stronger than Death: Hart Crane's Last Year in Mexico*

"Melissa Lee-Houghton's language is at once powerful, illuminating and pinging with beauty and pain. It pins down for us each particle that makes up an existence and like an electron spinning around its atom, *Exposure / Ideal Palace* is charged with endless possibilities. I'm not sure I ever want to recover from its sheer brilliance." **LEE ROURKE** · author of *Vantablack* and *Glitch*

"Two books in one: the first in free verse with a grounded narrative voice, the second more formally regular but wildly surreal. This is a phenomenally ambitious project and it's credit to the poet that there are so few missteps, given its consistently electrifying emotional pitch. Reading it feels like passing through a loud, unpredictable, hyperstimulating inferno, led by a reassuringly witty Virgil. Lee-Houghton has achieved something unique, and worth experiencing." **DAVE COATS** · Poetry Book Society

"The waves of words and sentences and all the telling of a life or lives on the pages and in the places where no-one waits or too many are present, where anger and desire meet, rise and fall and fail. There is sly humour, because, well, you have to laugh even when feeling pretty broken, on the floor in a coffee shop, for instance. There is sleeping and not sleeping and living and almost dying and fucking and being fucked, and there's waking up, every day, you know, despite it all. And there is leaving, because sometimes you can't stay, because you're not here, and you are out of options, because no-one sleeps next to the ravine, she writes, then asks if they do, and I had forgotten that part of it. I walked away from reading this book and then I came back, endless return to the stories that just do not stop, sometimes cut off, ending mid-sentence, to resume, darling, sweetheart, honey, a trail of endearments. And if you return once, she writes, you know what it is to return." **SHARON KIVLAND** · author of *Freud on Holiday* and *A Case of Hysteria*